HOW TO READ YOUR BIBLE

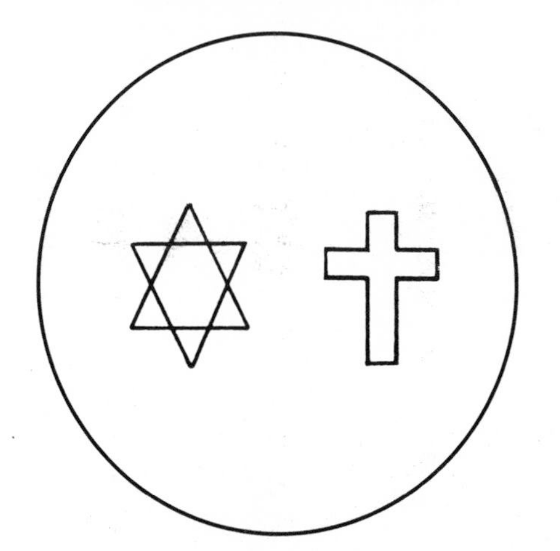

FRANCIS L. FILAS, S.J., S.T.D.

IMPRIMI POTEST:	Daniel L. Flaherty, S.J., Provincial Chicago Province of the Society of Jesus
NIHIL OBSTAT:	Thomas Aquinas Collins, O.P. Sr. Helen C. O'Neill, O.P. Diocesan Reviewers
	Thomas G. Doran Censor Deputatus
IMPRIMATUR:	+ Arthur J. O'Neill, D.D. Bishop of Rockford
Date:	August 9, 1978

The Nihil obstat and Imprimatur are official declarations that a book or pamphlet is free of doctrinal or moral error. No implication is contained therein that those who have granted the Nihil obstat and Imprimatur agree with the contents, opinions, or statements expressed.

Printed by:
Strathmore Company
Geneva, Illinois, U.S.A.

Cogan Productions
A Division of ACTA Foundation
11134 Youngtown Ave.
Youngtown, Arizona 85363

TABLE OF CONTENTS

PAGE:

HOW TO READ YOUR BIBLE

FOREWORD

These pages were written to provide a serious popularization of mature scripture study. They are intended to be a non-technical summary of key questions concerning the Bible in general, and selected biblical passages in particular. The approach is definitely "middle-of-the-road," avoiding on the one hand rigid fundamentalist literalism, and in the other direction, extreme negative scriptural opinions. While insisting on intellectual emphasis, this book is planned above all to be devotional, respectful and positive, following faithfully the principles of the monumental encyclical of Pius XII, *Divino Afflante Spiritu,* "On Holy Scripture."

Many developments have occurred since that encyclical was issued. The convocation of the Second Vatican Council resulted in a major reassessment of biblical studies, continuing along the guide lines of Pope Pius. Concurrently, new evidence from the Dead Sea Scrolls at Qumran and the Murabba'at shed new light on the culture that existed at the time of Jesus. Another revolutionary find at Ebla promises spin-off value in corroborating life conditions referred to in the Genesis stories of the patriarchs.

Factors like these, plus the Vatican II support of the ecumenical movement, have led to a common inter-religious interest in the Bible. The "Old" Testament has come to be studied more by Christians as the "Hebrew" Testament in its own right as the Word of God, and not merely or exclusively as a preparation for the New Testament of Jesus Christ. The discussions of Jesus with the Pharisees have been evaluated anew, more as family quarrels than the instant radical schism accepted by so many later centuries.

On the one hand, the extreme scepticism of the late Nineteenth Century biblical scholars has come to be rejected more and more, in view of the new knowledge of biblical cultures and biblical languages. On the other hand, the human element in the Bible has come to be accepted more and more, in the understanding that the inspiration of God cooperated with human conditions and human writers, with no detriment to either the human or the divine.

Thus, we offer these pages as a simplified, selective commentary on the two Testaments. We recommend that introductory sections be read first, in order to assimilate the principles behind a collection so complex and diverse as the biblical writings. Minor portions of the unit on the Old Testament have been adapted from ACTA Foundation's earlier *Guide to the Old Testament;* otherwise, all material has been developed originally so that this book would lead to a more penetrating study, deeper analysis, and more keen appreciation of the lifetime treasure that is our Bible.

Francis L. Filas, S.J., S.T.D.
Professor of Theology
Loyola University of Chicago

Unit I. Introduction

(a) The Place

The more vividly you can realize the locations and the distances involved in the stories of the Bible, so much the more easily will you understand (and be interested in) the Bible. Simplified, easy-to-read maps occur in this Guide. Use them!

For practical purposes, you can remember that most of the activity of the Hebrew (Old) and Greek (New) Testament occurred in what was called Palestine. This was a strip of land at the eastern end of the Mediterranean, about 150 miles from north to south, and 20 to 50 miles east from the Mediterranean to the Jordan River, the Dead Sea, and the southern desert.

The climate ranges from sub-tropical to desert to chilly rainy season, as can be felt at the Lake of Galilee (700 feet below sea level), the Dead Sea (1300 feet below sea level), and Jerusalem (3500 feet above sea level).

Outside Palestine, other countries encountered less prominently in the Bible are Egypt to the southwest; Babylon-Assyria to the east (modern Iraq and Iran); Asia Minor (for the early Christian Church, and for the homeland of nomads two thousand years earlier who wandered south into Palestine); and Greece and Italy (for Paul and early Christianity).

(b) The Time

The Bible comes to life perhaps even more when you can place each event in its proper sequence. You will find that it is both easier and more advantageous for you to do this: Know only a few important dates well. This is better than trying to get a surface acquaintance with many dates which are less relevant and less important. Here is a simplified chart of the main events in the Hebrew and Greek Testaments:

Hebrew Testament dates

About 1900 B.C.—The times of Abraham and succeeding biblical patriarchs.

About 1300 B.C.—The exodus of the Jewish slaves from Egypt, and the crossing of the Reed (accurately, *not* the "Red") Sea.

About the middle 1200's B.C.:—The progressive invasion of Canaanite Palestine by Joshua, leading the Israelites. This was followed by the period of the Judges.

1020 B.C. to 931 B.C.—The three Jewish kings in the united monarchy: Saul, David, and Solomon.

931 B.C.—The united monarchy splits up with a rebellion of the ten tribes forming the northern kingdom of Israel; and the two tribes forming the southern kingdom of Juda.

721 B.C.—Destruction of the northern kingdom of Israel by Assyria. Deportation of the survivors to such an extent that the "ten tribes" as such disappear from history.

587 B.C.—Destruction of the southern kingdom of Juda, this time by the Babylonians, followed by the exile to Babylon for about fifty years. This is a major turning-point in biblical history, referred to as "The Exile." From this time forward, Jews were dispersed into many other countries (the Jews of the "diaspora").

About 538 B.C.—Some of the exiles return from Babylon to rebuild Jerusalem, now conquered by the Persians. From here to 63 B.C., Palestine, for practical purposes, is under foreign domination except for a period of semi-independence after the revolt of the Maccabees in 160 B.C.

63 B.C.—The Roman general Pompey takes Jerusalem, partially as a pacifying influence to overcome warring Jewish factions.

Greek Testament Dates

Remember that for five hundred years into the Christian era, the years were still counted according to the Roman custom of "A.U.C.," *ab urbe condita,* the years from the legendary time of the founding of Rome. The changeover into "A.D." *(anno Domini,* "the year of the Lord") was made in the early 500's by a Benedictine monk, Dionysius Exiguus, who calculated the date of the birth of Christ erroneously. His mistake cannot be rectified even today because we do not have enough information. The dates suggested here for the life of Christ are considered most likely, but cannot be off by more than two or three years.

8 B.C.—Perhaps a Roman Census, referred to in the Christmas story, and announced at this time.

Spring, 6 B.C.—The birth of Jesus Christ.

April, 4 B.C.—The certain date of the death of Herod the Great. The report of his death is linked with an eclipse of the moon visible at Jericho, where he died. Such an eclipse occurred at this time.

27 A.D.—The beginning of the public ministry of Jesus.

Early April, 30 A.D.—The crucifixion, death, and resurrection of Jesus.

After 36 A.D.—The conversion of St. Paul.
45-49, 50-53, 54-58 A.D.—Paul's three missionary journeys.
58 A.D.—Paul's arrest at Jerusalem, leading to his confinement at Rome in 61-63 A.D.
About 64 A.D.—The martyrdom of St. Peter at Rome.
About 67 A.D.—The martyrdom of St. Paul at Rome.
70 A.D.—The capture and destruction of Jerusalem by Titus, after a three-year siege. This is an extremely important date. The destruction of Jerusalem wiped out earlier cultures and customs so thoroughly that no one later could have recorded these details of the past unless that person had been directly or indirectly in contact with eye-witness experience of the years before 70.

(c) The book and its authors: divine and human

The word "bible" simply means in Greek, "the writings." However, "bible" long ago acquired a very special meaning. It referred to that group of writings which, first from Jewish and then from Christian authority, were considered as having somehow originated from God. The essential point of the doctrine is that God is author of the Bible.

This divine authorship has never been spelled out in detail, even though it is a Roman Catholic dogma. If you are Catholic, you should note that from the viewpoint of your faith, you may freely accept any one of the many explanations offered to describe how God is "author." From the viewpoint of scholarship, you could hardly say with justification that God dictated the Bible word for word. The reason is this: the evidence is overwhelming that many human writers participated in this work. They were acting fully as human authors. Even more, from snatches here and there, it would appear that they did not feel aware of any divine influence upon them.

This does not mean that the divine influence did not exist. The religious doctrine remains that God wanted these writings to be. Somehow or other, God cooperated specially in bringing them to be. This divine cooperation is the foundation of all theories of inspiration, although biblical experts may differ as to how God is fully an "author."

Notice that "inspiration" is not the same thing as "revelation." In revelation from God, humans learn truths they would otherwise not have known on their own. In the case of the Bible, the evidence proves that many facts and opinions came from ordinary human sources such as court records, eye-witness accounts, popular epic poems, and ancestral traditions.

Notice, too, that the doctrine of the inspiration of the Bible does not mean that you must know why some particular writing came to be included in the biblical collection. Do not ask yourself, "What usefulness does this writing have for me?" as a norm to prove or indicate inspiration. That question traps you in a blind alley. You will find an apparent hodge podge of history, scraps of battle songs, poems, family trees, legal codes, short stories, prophecies, political speeches, even a fable. Long ago, it was quite evident that the unique norm for inspiration had to be the acceptance of biblical writing by a valid religious authority. No other norm can work. In the case of the Bible, that authority was the Christian church community, following upon the group acceptance by its Jewish spiritual ancestors.

Some persons claimed that they could use other norms to determine whether or not parts of the Bible were inspired. You can see at a glance that none of the norms proposed could be considered sufficient, whether individually or as a group: Does the Bible evoke in you holy thoughts? Does the Bible arouse repentance in you for your sins? Does biblical reading make you feel the impulse of the Holy Spirit? Is the antiquity of the Bible a sufficient reason for saying that God must be its author?

This cooperation of God in influencing the Bible must always remain a mystery to us, because all of God's actions on mankind are beyond our comprehension. Hence, we accept this fact that God is somehow the author of the Bible.

We turn now to the other part of the historical fact: Men were also in their own human way the authors of this book.

(d) The Bible is a "layer cake"

Again we run into complications, although not as incomprehensible as those concerned with the divine action. Who qualifies as a human author? Literary slaves often took the dictation and chose the words; should they be considered? Must the author be that man whose name is attached to the book? Fortunately for us, the answer does not concern any question of religious doctrine. Strictly speaking, it is not even a question of religious importance what men participated in writing a biblical book; whether they are known to us; whether they are anonymous; or whether they appear under someone else's name (called "pseudonymity") as was quite a custom in literary antiquity.

What do we mean by saying that the Bible is a "layer cake"? This phrase refers to the fact that our Bible represents only the finished product, the top layer, as it were. First came the contents of oral tradition; then some special parts of the tradition were selectively emphasized; then perhaps other source material was added; finally some or all of this material was put into writing. We have no direct way of knowing what re-writing and editing later occurred. One very important conclusion results: In some cases, our Bible faithfully reflects an early tradition but perhaps at one of the tradition's *later* stages, not necessarily its earliest.

You should remember not to expect an exactness of wording in the Bible that could come only from a transcribing of tape-recorded accounts. The biblical accounts are more faithful to what we could call the substance or general drift of speeches and descriptions of events.

(e) What do the words of the Bible MEAN?

One of the mistakes made by readers of the Bible has been to forget that the biblical writers wrote like men of their day, using phrases which had specific meaning for them. These phrases might be unknown to us because we are separated by hundreds of years and thousands of miles from their times and places. None the less, the biblical authors were writing the truth in their own way, even though we moderns might express this truth differently today in our own way.

The understanding of this fact leads us to try to find the "literary forms" in which the Bible was written. Literary forms are the expressions which convey the meanings an author intended his words to have.

Pope Pius XII put his authority behind the interpretation of the Bible according to its literary forms. The words of Pope Pius in his 1943 encyclical on holy scripture *(Divino Afflante Spiritu)* are a cogent argument against taking the words of the Bible in a slavishly literal sense.

"What is the literal sense of a passage is not always as obvious in the speeches and writings of the ancient authors of the East as it is in the works of our own time. For what they wished to express is not to be determined by the rules of grammar nor solely by the context. The interpreter must go back in spirit to those remote centuries of the past, and with the aid of history and other sciences, accurately determine what modes of writing the authors of that ancient period would be likely to use and in fact did use.

"No one who has a correct idea of biblical inspiration will be surprised to find even in the sacred writers as in other ancient authors, certain fixed ways of expounding and narrating, certain definite idioms, especially of a kind peculiar to the Semitic tongue, so-called approximations. Not infrequently, when some persons reproachfully charge the sacred writers with some historical error or inaccuracy in the recording of facts, on closer examination it turns out to be nothing else than those customary modes of expression peculiar to the ancients."

In other words, what a word says in the Bible is not necessarily what the word means in the Bible. If we moderns want our words to be understood for what they mean, and not just for what they say, then in fairness we should try to find what the words of the Bible mean, not merely what the words of the Bible say.

Consider just a few samples of modern literary forms we use today, which we definitely do not wish to be understood in their slavishly literal sense:

"My head is splitting with a headache."
"He is head over heels in love."
"I told my children a thousand times to be quiet."
"Everybody (or nobody) came to the party."

The local newspaper is a storehouse of more. The same phrase has a different meaning, depending on where it appears in the paper. A want-ad says that a bargain is a "steal." The sports page gives credit to the fast runner in baseball for "stealing home." On another page, a man is reported sent to prison for fraud because he did precisely that: he stole a home!

Just to give a very few examples from the Bible: "Fire from heaven" means lightning. The long genealogies of Genesis listing great ages are not interested in claiming that these people actually lived so long. They want instead to make the point symbolically that these were the great ancestors of old. "All the people with one voice shouted" is certainly an approximation and a summary of a majority opinion.

One instance excellently illustrates how our modern ignorance of past customs can make us grossly misunderstand the meaning of an ancient allusion. For centuries, the phrase, "to consult the Lord" (as in I Samuel 23:2) was popularly considered to mean some sort of prayer David offered to God, to find God's will. Only in later times was it learned that "consulting the Lord" actually meant casting lots. This was done by means of the *Urim* and *Thummim,* which were either sacred dice, sticks, or stones carried in a box by the priest.

(f) How the biblical text has come down to us.

The knowledge of how the Bible was written and completed twenty and more centuries ago still leaves a major question unanswered. How do we know that our text of the Bible reads correctly? The objection is very logical. Any document which has been copied and re-copied so many hundreds of times, over so many centuries, must be riddled with errors made by the copyists. How then could it be considered reliable?

A confident answer comes from what is called the science of textual criticism. This study emphasizes that all human documents are copied according to an identical pattern. The copyists tend to make the same mistakes, whether deliberately (to try to clear up some obscure passages) or indeliberately (from fatigue or lack of attention). Very importantly, these copyists can never make the same mistakes at the same places. In the case of the thousands of biblical manuscrips, copied over so many centuries in so many countries, no one could possibly have reached all these copyists and persuaded them to write an identical false text. Spontaneously, these copyists did their best. When they made their mistakes (the same mistakes you and I make—such as misspelling and doubling words or omitting them), the mistakes occur at different places. By comparing the manuscripts, the scholars can notice the mistaken letters or words standing out like the proverbial sore thumb. Thus, the scholars can conclude to the bulk of the material, which is truly copied correctly.

We are positively certain that the textual readings of the Hebrew and Greek Testaments are far more than 99% correct, in reproducing the wordings from centuries ago. A hitherto unknown Hebrew manuscript of the Prophet Isaiah, found among the Qumran Dead Sea scrolls, reads just about the way the scholars deduced it should read. Yet, before the 1947 find at Qumran, the only Hebrew Isaiah text was from a thousand years after the time of Qumran. This was a wholly unexpected confirmation of the techniques of the science of textual criticism.

Why is the so-called Protestant and Jewish Hebrew Testament shorter than the so-called Catholic Bible? The first point to note is that the terms "Protestant Bible" and "Catholic Bible" are falling more and more into disuse. Instead the terms, "Hebrew text" and "Greek text" or "Septuagint" of the Hebrew (Old) Testament are being substituted. (The New Testament is not in question on this point). The historical reasons for the differences are these:

After the Babylonian exile in the 500's B.C., Jews spread all over the then-known world. As time went on, they lost more and more contact with their ancestral Hebrew tongue, and therefore with their religious traditions. Since Greek was the universal language of culture, a translation of the existing Bible was gradually made at Alexandria in Egypt some time in the 200's B.C. This Greek translation was dubbed the "Septuagint," from the Latin word for "seventy." A legend had been invented in order to give the new Greek translation public acceptance. Supposedly, seventy men did the translation separately, and all seventy "miraculously" came up with the same version. The legend of course was false, but the name for "70" has remained in history for the Greek translation of the Hebrew Testament.

The first Christians, Jewish as they were, consistently used this Septuagint version. After the fall of Jerusalem in 70 A.D., Jewish rabbis consulted as to how to hold the almost destroyed nation together. They decided to reclassify the authentic books of the Bible. They excluded some of the more recent books of the Septuagint as being not Hebrew enough or as written outside Palestine or as failing to conform with Mosaic tradition. This led to a shorter list. Fifteen centuries later, the Protestant Reformers adopted this shorter list as well. Meanwhile, the Catholic Church considered the longer list of books as inspired, even though some doubts had been expressed. The Council of Trent settled the issue against the Reformers.

Nowadays, all scholars readily admit that the books of the Septuagint represent the earlier and more primitive list of the Hebrew canon ("canon" is the technical term for the list of inspired books in the Bible). Modern Bibles issued under non-Catholic auspices often include the books dropped from the Septuagint under the heading, "The Apocrypha," and place them in an appendix. Catholic doctrine continues to look on them as equally inspired with the rest of the Bible.

Unit 2. The Old Testament

BEFORE YOU BEGIN READING GENESIS

In a planned approach to reading the Bible, there is something of a decision to be made: Should I read my Bible in the order in which I find the books printed there, or should I read it according to the most probable chronological order of the books?

There is much to be said in favor of following the biblical development of themes in the order in which they were written. You can see there something of the growth of an idea from incompleteness to a fuller meaning. However, you will meet many more difficulties if you try to follow this "chronological" approach. At best, your reading is chopped up, as you are forced to skip from here to there and then back again somewhere else. You are also subject to the fact that no one can actually tell you with complete certainty when each part of the Bible was written. Remember what we said earlier about the Bible being a "layer cake." In some cases scholars can give you conclusive evidence of the dates of authorship. In most cases, these dates cannot be made precise but rest instead between outside limits.

In the following pages we will follow the Old and New Testaments in the order in which the books are printed there. You should remember throughout that this order is sometimes completely at variance with the times of the events described.

The Pentateuch

The first five books of the Old Testament have been called for centuries the *Pentateuch,* or *Torah.* "Pentateuch" is the English equivalent of the Greek words, *penta* and *teuchos,* "five scrolls." "Torah" is the English transliteration of the Hebrew word for "law" or "way of life." These five books are Genesis, Exodus, Leviticus, Numbers, and Deuteronomy.

One of the characteristics you will soon find in reading these works is the recurrence of similar and almost exact stories sometimes attributed to different persons in different places and times. These similar stories were long called "doublets" or "triplets," depending on the number of repetitions.

Even in the English translated from the Hebrew you will also notice the differences of style: some accounts are warm and detailed, others are dry narratives, using stereotyped phrases again and again.

If you were able to read the original Hebrew, you would also notice that God is referred to by different names: sometimes the "Lord," (*Yahweh* in Hebrew), sometimes "God" (*Elohim* in Hebrew.)

These and other differences led scholars to conclude that the five books of the Pentateuch originated out of at least four main traditions. One tradition was called "Jahwist" or "Yahwist," (abbreviated *J,* from the German spelling, *Jahve,* "Lord"); another was called "Elohist" (abbreviated *E,* because it characteristically referred to God as *Elohim);* another was called "Deuteronomic" (abbreviated *D,* because it was apparently written by the historian author of the book of Deuteronomy); and the last was called "Priestly" (abbreviated *P,* because it originated with the priestly community connected with the temple at Jerusalem).

All of these have been traced back to certain centuries for their approximate origins. The oldest is the Jahvist, from the 900's B.C.; next in age is the Elohist, from the northern part of the Holy Land in about the 700's B.C.; next, the Deuteronomic, from the 600's; and finally the Priestly, the most recent, from the 400's B.C.

As you read Genesis and the other books of the Pentateuch, you should keep in mind that these works are mosaics, wherein the four great traditions are skillfully intertwined. The men who put these books together were not concerned about possible discrepancies in the stories from one tradition compared with the same stories in another tradition. Instead, the Bible faithfully reproduces the traditions as its authors came to know them in their own times. This already is a partial answer to the accusation that the Bible is loaded with contradictions. The Bible's faithfulness to its sources is indicated all the more by its retention of all its traditions, even while recognizing the discrepancies among these traditions.

The Book of Genesis

FOR READING GENESIS, Chapters 1 through 11.

We now take up what is without doubt one of the greatest religious documents of all time. In eleven short chapters of the Book of Genesis you will find one of the most sublime descriptions of the very heart and soul of religion. The portrait of God sketched in Genesis encompasses the fact that God is "wholly other"—completely beyond us—and shows God's tender concern and condescension for His creature, man. Man is presented in all his dignity and glory as well as in his wretchedness without God. These chapters are not merely a statement of the religious facts of life. They are also a ringing appeal to all men and women to live up to their great vocation of being made in God's image and likeness.

The first eleven chapters of Genesis are radically different from what follows them. Strictly speaking, they are not presenting "history" in the way that later chapters present Abraham and the other biblical patriarchs. They are a literary link with the Chosen People, to connect them with God's very creation. Some of the elements in these accounts (as, for example, Chapters 2 and 3 on man and woman in the Garden) go back to 900 B.C. from the Yahwistic tradition. Others, like the Priestly account in Chapter 1 (the six days of creation) go back to the 400's B.C.

But scholars agree that the traditions are far, far older than these written forms. Many of the images and expressions used are taken from the common folklore of the people of the Middle East. The authors, you must remember, were people of their time. So were their hearers when these tales were told and retold in the tents of desert nomads.

What is the Genesis story?

We might call it an argument in poetic and imaginative language. The authors say to the pagan world around them, "You are wrong! The world is not an accident, nor is it something evil. It is the carefully planned work of the one true God." Genesis was composed to set the people straight on basic religious questions of life. The authors are very anxious to arm their people against the fantastic explanations of the origin of man and of the universe which were current among their pagan neighbors.

Here it is necessary to point out one extremely important distinction. Again and again, the Bible uses pagan words and refers to pagan religious customs; but *always,* the Bible "baptizes" these expressions, as it were, to change their significance so that they can be rightly understood only in the context of adoring and obeying the one true God. The "tree of life," for example, is taken from such pagan imagery; so are the "cherubim", originally demi-gods or guardian spirits in pagan mythology. The very name for God, "El," was sometimes used for pagan gods.

Sometimes, the biblical writer uses these pagan expressions as a kind of hidden polemic to ridicule the false religions. It has been logically suggested that the "serpent" in Chapter 3 of Genesis symbolizes the fertility cults, as opposed to the one true God. The meaning would be that the source of all evil and suffering can be traced to desertion of the one true God by means of adherence to nature (and ultimately, man) as one's god.

In other words, the imagery is stripped of all its pagan trappings. The symbols may be retained, but their symbolism is drastically and radically altered.

Some pagans thought that the world and mankind were an accident, a mere by-product of a war among the gods. Others looked upon the material world as the creation of an evil god, and the world of spirit was the handiwork of a good god. (This belief in the existence of two equal gods of good and of evil is called "dualism.") In contrast to these various explanations, the account of Genesis has been universally acclaimed as one of the world's masterpieces of literature for its sublimity, its beauty, and its dignified tone.

The problems of Genesis

1. Was the world created in the way that the authors of Genesis describe the creation?

No. God, through collaboration with the human authors, was trying to put across in a simple, easily understood way the basic truths of man's destiny and purpose of life. The audience was a primitive, simple group of nomads. Genesis described things to them in a non-scientific way, as the universe appears to the senses, not as it exists in its ultimate explanations.

These people had no telescopes, no microscopes, no computers, only their eyes and ears. We ourselves are unable to reach the ultimate explanations, even though we have the telescopes, microscopes, and computers.

2. Is the story of Genesis a true story?

Yes, if we take the author on his own terms, and if we accept the truth the author intends to give us. To understand what the author is saying, we must put out of our minds such questions as, "Did God really create the world in six periods of twenty-four hours each?" "Was there a real tree, and what kind of fruit did our first parents eat?" We must approach the account in a truly objective manner and ask the proper questions: "What is the message of Genesis?"

3. What is the message of Genesis?
   a. There is only one God, and everything depends on Him. Even the great sun and moon, so awe-inspiring that many men had turned to them in worship, were God's handiwork.
   b. God is all-powerful, and the author brings this out by describing by a mere word of command, "God spoke, and it was so."
   c. God is the God of order and harmony. Though man is one of the smallest of God's creatures, he is the one of the most important, because mankind was made in the image and likeness of God, in a very special way.

The Two Accounts of Creation

As you begin to read, notice the completely different styles in chapter 1, compared to chapters 2 and 3. Chapter 1 places the framework of creation within the seven-day week, so that the work of six days of creation is crowned with the rest of the Sabbath—a literary way of teaching the importance of Sabbath observance, as if even God observed it from the beginning. Chapters 2 and 3 on the other hand are extremely "human," as it were, manifesting clever psychological insights into typical male and female temperament, and leading to the existence of a primal disobedience to God as the source of suffering and death. The lessons in the two traditions are the same, but the literary frameworks, the styles, the outlooks, the emphasis are all different. Some outstanding lessons are these:

1) God exists;
2) God is one;
3) God is good;
4) God made all creation;
5) Creation is therefore good;
6) Creation should not be adored as if it were a god.

Highpoints of These Selections

In reading the creation story, you must always keep in mind that the authors of Genesis were not philosophers. Abstract ideas like "nothingness" had no meaning for them. The closest they could come to an idea of producing something where nothing had existed before (creation), was to describe it as a putting into order of the vast chaos that had earlier existed. They visualized chaos as darkness and wild waters; we ourselves cannot do much better when we try to imagine what nothingness must be or "not be."

GENESIS, Chapter 1:

Again and again the pages of Genesis say that "God saw that it was good." This was partially to refute the dualistic religions holding to a good and an evil god, and partially to refute the idea that matter itself was evil. Nothing that God has made is bad in itself. Evil depends upon how much man exercises his dominion, and how he does it.

Far from letting the heavenly bodies be gods in themselves, Genesis places the sun and moon and stars to serve mankind, to act as aids to navigation, to provide light and warmth, although even in this the outlook is not that of modern science. Light as such is looked on as if it were a sort of thin liquid, independent of the heavenly bodies. The sun and moon and stars are significantly relegated only to the fourth day of creation, to show that they are subordinate to the one true God. They have no right to be adored in themselves.

Notice in Chapter 1 how "male and female" are explicitly described in an exultant hymn-like chant, far different from the pattern of the "ordinary" creation of the rest of the universe.

GENESIS, Chapter 2:

Compared to the Chapter 1 of the Priestly writers, the Chapter 2 of the Yahwistic author presents a completely different environment within which creation should be visualized. The "garden" is actually an oasis in the desert, with plentiful water. Little attention is paid to the creation of the inanimate or animal universe. All the action centers around man and woman. God is pictured as if God were a potter, making man out of clay. God makes woman from a part of man in a superb passage that presents several vital teachings:

1) Man loses something of his fullness of human nature, which woman now possesses, so that either sex in itself is psychologically incomplete.

2) Man has received the breath of God, which gave man his unique rights as a human, made in the image of God. Woman does not have a separate creation, but shares this divine image as "partitioned" from man.

3) Marriage is the coming together of these two incompletes, so that man and woman complete and fill out each other as spouses.

One technical term should be explained at this point, since it is so often mentioned in connection with the Yahwistic writer. The Yahwist is very "anthropomorphic." This word means that he pictures God as if God were a human being, acting in human ways. God forms man from clay, God converses with Adam and Eve, God takes a walk in the afternoon.

We ourselves find it impossible to speak about God without using "anthropomorphisms." The Bible has to use them constantly. The most common anthropomorphism (meaning "in the likeness of man") is the reference to God as "he" or as our "father." Strictly speaking, it is no more incorrect to call God "she" than it is to call God "he." We have no adequate pronoun to accomplish the task. Certainly, as creator, God possesses in Himself all qualities preeminently of maleness and femaleness, but Genesis here looks on God as fatherly.

You might also wonder at this point about the highly misunderstood controversy whether or not the Bible teaches the evolution of the human body.

The answer has to be that the Bible simply does not discuss the fact. It is neither for nor against the purely scientific theory of the origin of higher forms of life from lower forms. Its only interest is to make the one great point: God made human beings. Precisely how God made them is a question even we do not know today, with all our science. The Bible is not speaking in terms of knowing the scientific theory, but suggests these vivid pictures as a popular way to visualize the action of God.

Someone once made the acute observation that the Bible could only be against atheistic evolution. But evolution that is atheistic is no longer natural science. Atheistic evolution is a philosophy that tries to explain human life without the influence of God. Anything that outlaws God is contrary to Genesis.

GENESIS, Chapter 3:

Here the author explains the fall of man in a way which takes into account that vague feeling in every person's heart that there was once some terrible calamity that altered the course of history and brought in its wake suffering and death. The psychological process of temptation outlined here is a masterpiece of sensitive and acute observation of human nature.

What was the sin of the man and the woman, as described in Chapter 3? It certainly is not pictured as a sin of sexual intercourse. Such an interpretation would be a puritanical violation of the basic goodness of the creation God had made for this husband and wife. Fundamentally, it is a deliberate act of disobedience that can be reduced to a refusal to accept God. In that sense it becomes idolatry of self.

It is a different question to ask precisely in what terms the genius of the Genesis author indicates this sin. Many scholars see here an underlying polemic against the Canaanite fertility cults. This would mean that the sin is detailed as if a believer in the Lord Yahweh frequented the Canaanite temple prostitutes, in the attempt to obtain fertile crops by his imitative "fertility" actions—a sort of "sympathetic magic." At this early point in your Bible reading, you should accustom yourself to recognize the biblical attacks against the fertility cults. The Bible looks on these cults as idolatrous insults to the one true God. Nature in them is treated as a god. Such blasphemy Genesis cannot bear, like the prophets in later biblical pages.

GENESIS, Chapter 4:

Following close upon the fall of man comes a second sin, the first murder. The author's first readers—or listeners—were desert wanderers who were quite familiar with the constant struggle and rivalry between shepherds and settled farmers. It was in this context that the spread of sin is described.

Earlier, we held that the literary form of the Book of Genesis indicates that these stories were to teach a lesson rather than to be taken as modern history or geology or astronomy. In the same way, the linking of Cain and Abel as the direct children of Adam and Eve is what is called a literary link, not a claim of direct blood descent. The stories are joined, to continue the lesson that one sin leads to another. Are the stories true? They certainly are, in the sense we mentioned previously, "If we take the author on his own terms, and if we accept the truth which the author intends to give us."

GENESIS, Chapter 5:

This chapter is your first encounter with genealogies in the Bible. Perhaps nowhere else is it more imperative to remember that the literary forms of the past can be vastly different in meaning from the connotations we would attach to them. There can be no reasonable historical doubt that Genesis imitates the customs of neighboring nations in ascribing great ages to its ancestors. Genesis, in fact, is restrained in comparison to the 65,000-year lifetimes attributed to the kings of other peoples. The meaning here is definitely symbolic. Scholars still argue what the symbolism must be, but we must conclude that the Bible does not teach that mankind once lived to ages ten times as much as the present average.

GENESIS, Chapter 6 through Chapter 9:

In the story of the flood, we are shown to what depths of sin and degradation the human race can sink when it becomes alienated from God. Scholarly study tells us that the way in which the authors depict the terrible calamity does not mean that there was an actual, worldwide deluge. Stupendous miracles upon miracles would be called for to accomplish such a feat (e.g., the mixing of salt and sea water, the gathering of animals from all weather zones, the fact that the animals in the ark would be food for each other!). Instead, the flood story takes the frequent experience of damaging floods to teach its lessons: God's justice must not permit sin to go unpunished, but God's mercy will permit weak and sinful man, in the hope of conversion, to continue to live. If ever you are inclined to read the literary forms of the flood narrative in Genesis in slavishly literal fashion, you will meet still another difficulty: the statistics of *two* flood stories are intermingled again and again. Biblical study identifies one of these accounts as the P (Priestly) tradition, and the other as the J (Yahwistic) tradition. These statistics, if taken literally, would contradict each other. Hence, all the evidence points to a symbolic interpretation of the flood story, consistent with the symbolid interpretation of the rest of the first eleven chapters of Genesis. That interpretation culminates in the powerful lesson: God is merciful to sinful, vacillating man!

Here for the first time we suggest the fallacy of that common saying that the Hebrew Old Testament is the law of fear, but the New Testament is supposedly the law of love. You must remember (and you will yourself notice this easily) the repeated teachings of God's love and mercy in the Old Testament. In the New Testament, you will notice later that Jesus of necessity must mention God's justice as well as God's love.

GENESIS, Chapter 11:

In the story of the Tower of Babel, the last of the "teaching stories" of the first eleven Genesis chapters, you find man again attempting to exercise his dominion apart from God. As background to the story of the Tower of Babel, imagine the long lasting impression which the great commercial and trading centers made on the little bands of Israelite nomads. The high temple platforms, called "ziggurats," erected by the Babylonians to their gods, symbolized the height of man's conceited refusal to accept the one true God. The Tower of Babel story is an effective antidote against that atheistic self-reliance. Do not be concerned about the fact that the framework of the story concerns the supposed origin of different languages in mankind. The biblical writers would no more expect their traditions to be a scientific explanation of the growth of languages than they would have expected the earlier creation stories to have been treatises in modern astro-physics.

READ: GENESIS, Chapters 12 through 25

The Beginnings of the Bible

The historical beginning of the Bible occurred almost four thousand years ago with a nomad sheik named Abraham. We read his story in Genesis, Chapters 12 through 25.

The whole of these chapters is very easy reading and well worth the time. Here we can touch upon only the main points. We know that the Bible dates the history of God's people from the day when Abraham heard God's call and answered with trusting faith.

Remember again that Genesis enters strictly historical times with this Chapter 12. The earlier chapters had been a literary link, teaching moral lessons of God's supremacy, goodness, justice, and love. In that sense they are out of time and are not dated.

But Abraham and the times of the patriarchs are definitely dated in their references to particular lands and particular cultures. Abraham's original home was "Ur of the Chaldees," a wealthy commercial center at the head of the Persian Gulf. Ur had a great temple dedicated to the moon-god. Abraham was a man of his time, first a worshipper of the gods of the Fertile Crescent. "Fertile Crescent" is the name given to lands which form the backdrop of nearly everything which happened in the Bible. If you draw a line from Egypt through Palestine and Syria and follow the Tigris River from the Euphrates Valley to the Persian Gulf, the result will be an unmistakable crescent-shaped line of fertile lands.

In Abraham's day (about 2000 B.C.), invading mountain people poured in from the north. Biblical scholars have suggested that the reason why Abraham moved may well have been his dissatisfaction with the religion of his homeland. At any rate, after leaving Ur, Abraham became a desert wanderer, living off the land with his clan and his flocks.

Notice in these chapters once again the recurrence of the doublet and even triplet narratives. These are usually evidence of the inclusion of the J (Yahwistic), P (Priestly), and E (Elohistic) tradition.

The great promises of God, first mentioned in Genesis, 12, 2-3, and then in 18, 18 and 22, 16-18, are consistent as they come down from the various traditions. They may be summed up in this way:

1) Abraham will have descendants more numerous than the stars;

2) Abraham's descendants will possess a kingdom;

3) This kingdom will be a source of all good things for the whole of mankind.

GENESIS, Chapter 12, 12-20:

We must pause for a moment to look more deeply into the question whether or not Abraham should be accused of a "moral failure" in lying that his wife was his sister, in order to save his life. The first point to note is that no question of faith is involved in the varying interpretations made of this passage. There are parallel passages where Abraham appears to lie in the same way to a king Abimelech, instead of the Egyptian pharaoh (Gen. 20, 1-17), and where Isaac appears to lie in the same way before this same king Abimelech (Gen. 26, 6-12). For long centuries through to our own day, the one interpretation had been that these were actually lies on the part of the patriarchs. It was thought that these men perhaps knew no better or that perhaps they actually were that cowardly and deceitful.

As early as the 1920's, archeological evidence offered a different solution to the puzzle. Ancient legal records now discovered and deciphered indicate that the culture at the time of Abraham preferred the "fratriarchal" system (brother to brother or sister) as the highest form of legal relationship. In that context, these very primitive traditions in Genesis were indeed accurate. They showed that both Abraham and Isaac bestowed on their wives a *higher* legal relationship by "adopting" their wives as their legal sisters.

But what evidently happened in later centuries was that this custom died out and became unknown. Further traditions then felt obliged to interpret the primitive traditions before them as if the patriarchs had lied, since no other solution seemed possible. Thus it is that Genesis faithfully collects its traditional sources, without passing judgment on the accuracy of their interpretation.

GENESIS, Chapter 15:

The ancient ceremony for making contracts described here was for the parties of the agreement to pass through the divided parts of an animal. The meaning behind the act was, "Let what has happened to this animal happen to the first man who breaks this agreement." Certainly, the action of God in making a covenant with Abraham is described in a very anthropomorphic way.

GENESIS, Chapter 22:

There can be little doubt concerning the faith God asks of Abraham in the sacrifice of Isaac, the only chance Abraham could see for the promises of posterity to be fulfilled. In commanding such a sacrifice, God shows His supreme dominion over all life. In revoking the command, God shows that He does not wish men to express the recognition of His dominion by human sacrifice.

Mature and meditative reading of these Genesis passages can group their lessons around three key words: Call, Covenant, and Faith.

CALL: The whole of sacred history and of the life of each one of us depends entirely upon the initiative of God.

FAITH: But God has willed that His actions in history have a consequence in the lives of men. God calls on mankind for faith, but this is not some sort of arbitrary challenge, inexplicable as it may be from our present vantage point. God has His own good reasons.

COVENANT: The closeness and intimacy of God's activity with men and women is first expressed by the symbol of a covenant, a contract.

Every contract implies a unity between the participants, but not every contract is between equals, as in this case. This is the first of such images and symbols, later to be found in the union of bride and bridegroom.

READ: EXODUS, Chapters 2 through 14

The Book of Exodus

Understandably, we can make only representative selections in these pages to explain, as it were, typical passages of the Bible. The book of Exodus ranks high for its importance, because it recounts the providential interference of God to save His people from destruction.

What went before: Some nineteen or twenty centuries before Christ, Abraham had heard the call of Yahweh and received the promise from God. Isaac, the child of promise, passed this faith on to his son Jacob, who settled in the land of Goshen in the northeastern part of Egypt. This settlement occurred perhaps around 1700 B.C., under the protection of the Hyksos dynasty. However, the Hyksos Pharaohs were not truly Egyptian but Semitic. Thus it was that when the Egyptians threw off the foreign yoke under the Rameses, the Egyptians were not slow in punishing any former friends of their hated masters. This bit of history explains why the Jews first found a haven and then slavery in the land of Egypt.

With the appearance of Moses, the record of God's dealings with the tiny Israelite clan takes a decisive step. God in His providence will turn the unorganized band of refugees into one people. The time is about 1300 B.C.

The Call

EXODUS, Chapter 1:

It is interesting to note that the scene of the Call, Horeb or Sinai, the "mountain of the Lord," is the same as that of the giving of the Law. God is symbolically represented here by fire, a symbolism that is quite constant throughout the two Testaments.

EXODUS, Chapter 3:

The divine name, Yahweh, expresses the complete and perfect independence of God. The ancient Hebrews were not philosophers and probably did not see the metaphysical implications of the divine name. These Hebrews probably understood God's independence concretely in reference to His independent activity on behalf of His chosen people. But the fact remains that this personal name of God is closely connected with the verb, "to be," and we do not read too much into it when we understand God as one whose nature it is to exist, and who is in no way dependent on anyone else. You can summarize the biblical impression of God as "the wholly Other." That impression is no less correct in our own day.

EXODUS, Chapter 4:

The continual references to God's hardening Pharaoh's heart is due to the sacred writers' practice of looking to the primary cause of things, God, with a certain loss of emphasis on the secondary causes, in this case, Pharaoh's greed and pride.

The Hebrew expression might better be rendered, "Pharaoh became stubborn." To the Hebrew mind, when fruit fell from a tree in the orchard because of the law of gravity, the Hebrew would say that God had plucked the apple from the tree. This ultimately is not false, since the law of gravity remains an expression of the will of the Creator.

The Passover

EXODUS, Chapter 12:

Concerning the Passover meal, the details of the preparation of the lamb are significant. Roasting was the quickest way to prepare the lamb. Bitter herbs (probably wild endive and wild lettuce) pointed up the bitterness of oppression. The way in which the meal was to be eaten, with staff in hand, also indicated the hastiness and readiness for departure. The bread is unleavened, since there is no time to wait for the dough to rise.

EXODUS, Chapter 12:

How many Israelites left Egypt? Their number seems far too large to have passed by the ford in a single night. In another place we are told that the number of Israelites was too small to settle the whole of Palestine at one time. For these reasons it seems that the number given has been miscopied in the course of time.

EXODUS, Chapter 12: (into Chapter 13)

The "law of azymes (unleavened bread) and firstborn" was intended to be a perpetual reminder to the people of the great saving act of God which God had done for them on the eve of their escape from bondage.

EXODUS, Chapter 13, v. 16:

This verse is the origin of the custom of wearing "phylacteries," which were small leather boxes containing little scrolls upon which were written certain scriptural passages. These boxes were bound to the forehead and arm during prayer by leather thongs.

Any religious practice by anyone anywhere can be subject to abuse. It is easy to look down on this custom as ostentatious and hypocritical, but such a supercilious attitude forgets that the custom of external observances has a salutary psychological effect provided the essential interior motivation is not lost.

The Crossing

EXODUS, Chapter 14:

The Israelites were directed to take the longer route around the Sinai peninsula because this less traveled route would avoid the customs stations and garrisons of soldiers which abounded along the great coastal highway between Egypt and Canaan.

The exact method by which the Israelites crossed the Sea is uncertain, but the combination of circumstances which enabled them to make their escape was certainly providential to the point of being miraculous. In other words, the real miracle is not so much the precise way in which they crossed as in the fact that God provided this means of escape just at the moment when it was needed.

Notice that our present reading of crossing the "Red" Sea is a mistake. The Israelites probably crossed the "Reed" Sea, a group of marshy areas far to the north of the Red Sea, most likely the swamps near the Mediterranean coast.

The crossing of this Reed Sea by the Israelites was to make a great impression on future generations of Jews as is shown from the constant reference to it throughout the rest of scripture. It became for the Jews the great symbol of God's special care for His people. The individual Jew was freed from the bondage of Egypt precisely because he belonged to the people of God. The lesson of God's over-shadowing providence cannot be lost on all people of succeeding ages.

The Book of Deuteronomy

READ DEUTERONOMY, Chapter 4; Chapters 26 through 30.

The vocation of Moses was the vocation of Israel in miniature. That the place where Moses first heard the call of God and the place where Israel was to seal its covenant with God were one and the same (Mount Sinai) was no accident. It was Moses' mission to lead one people out of the misery of slavery. It was the mission of that people to be the channel of salvation for all men.

For the first time in our reading of the Bible, we come across one of its great themes, "The Law." This expression embodied for the pious

Israelite a way of life which if observed carefully assured him of God's favor. Since this idea of the Law, as encompassing a whole outlook on life, is so basic to an understanding of the Old Testament, it is worth our while to examine briefly the law of Moses.

In origin it drew upon the common law of the whole Middle East, but it has an elevated tone and spiritual quality which sets it far above other legal codes of its day. Its idea of justice might seem harsh to the modern reader, but it was quite merciful by the standard of its day. One of the most outstanding qualities of the Hebrew Law Code was its concern for the weak and defenceless, the widow and the orphan, and its insistence on the dignity of woman.

Its most unique quality is that it pictures God as above and beyond His creation. It totally rejected the view of other religions of the day. They confused or identified God with the forces of nature.

Israelite thought often placed the law in a historical framework. Sometimes a historical event will offer motives for obeying the law, or a practical application of the law, in order to make the particular law more meaningful to the people who are expected to observe it.

What is the message of Deuteronomy? This book which is cast in the form of a series of addresses or sermons of Moses to the people on the threshold of their entry into the promised land contains some of the most sublime words on true morality. Its message might be summed up in this way: love and righteousness go together. To love God also means to love and deal justly and uprightly with one's neighbor.

It tells of the one true God who is a LIVING God not wrought of wood or stone. He is a JEALOUS God in that He cannot remain indifferent when His people turn away from Him. He is a LOVING God in that He has exercised the most amazing providence in behalf of His chosen people. And he has chosen them not because they were the most numerous of the people of the earth, and not because they had always been His faithful servants, for just the opposite was often the case. He chose them because He had loved them and was determined to keep His promises to their fathers.

Notice that the people in their turn must FEAR God. But notice that the "fear of the Lord" (a phrase that will recur constantly in the wisdom literature of the Bible) means a loving reverence of God, not some sort of obsequious terror. Most of all, God's people should return LOVE for love. They must give God an intense, personal devotion which seeks to give undivided loyalty in every phase of life.

DEUTERONOMY, Chapter 4:

Again we can select only a few of the highpoints. Deuteronomy forms what might be called an inspired commentary on the events of the Exodus. It shows the meaning behind the events. It has been called the purest form of historical writing as the Jews understood this type of writing. For the Jews, historical writing was not a mere reporting of events and dates but rather an explanation of the significance of the events. We would look on this more as a philosophy or a theology of history.

The passage chosen here is one of the most beautiful in the entire book of Deuteronomy. It is a beautiful and eloquent expression of wonder at God's loving care for His people.

The repeated prohibition against representing God in some material form was to emphasize God's spiritual nature. Because of the pagan world of idolatry surrounding the Israelites, there was great danger of backsliding into idolatry, or of trying to assimilate the worship of the one true God into an idolatrous fertility cult.

It is striking to note that the book of Deuteronomy is quoted some thirty-two times in the New Testament, and with allusions and indirect quotations, it appears in some one hundred and twelve passages in the New Testament.

It is also from Deuteronomy that the biblical motto for the protection of life in the womb has been extracted:

"Choose Life!" (Deut. 30, 19)

READ: Book of Joshua, Chapters 1 through 7; 23 and 24.
Book of Judges, Chapter 2; Chapters 13 through 16.

Joshua and Judges

"God is faithful!" These words ring out down through the course of the Old Testament. In the two books you are now going to sample, Joshua and Judges, you will see how God acts with perfect fidelity in carrying out His promises. This is the main theme of the Book of Joshua. At the same time you will notice that the promised land was not handed to the Chosen People on a silver platter. The conquest of Canaan, the land flowing with milk and honey, was a long and bitter struggle. The people suffered defeat and virtual enslavement on many occasions.

Do not think that it is necessary to accept all the ruthlessness of Joshua as actually instigated and approved by God. When we consider the awful suffering involved in the conquest of Canaan, especially for the subjugated Canaanites, it raises a moral question that is painful and leads to uneasiness. How can we understand the conviction of the ancient

Israelites that God actually participated in their struggle? Yahweh appears almost as a "God of holy war," ruthlessly exacting the bloody extermination of Israel's enemies as tribute to Him. You must keep in mind that just because the Bible recounts all the warlike extremes of Joshua, this does not mean that the Bible automatically approves of each individual action, even though Joshua certainly approved.

Sometimes the answer has been suggested that if the Israelites had not pursued their enemies so ruthlessly, they themselves would have been tortured in the same manner. However, this does not solve the problem, even though it offers a mitigating factor. We must be content to mention the situation as a historical fact.

As for the Book of Judges, it was written to answer an objection. If God was as faithful to His promises as the sacred authors claimed, why was the possession of the Promised Land gained at such a terrible cost, and so transitory and uncertain a possession at best?

There are several other instructional themes running through Joshua and Judges. As you read through the assigned chapters (and others that you may want to pursue), see if you can pick examples of these themes:

1) The moral unity or solidarity of the community;

2) the will of God that all men be saved (and that Israel is not the only beneficiary of the divine plan);

3) the personal moral responsibility of the individual (that is, each member of the nation is to be judged on his own fidelity to the Covenant.)

Joshua, compared to Judges, might be called "Epic History." It paints with a broad brush, and touches only the highlights of a military campaign in Canaan. The emphasis is placed on the essential event: God has promised His people a land of their own, and now God fulfills His promise. Scholars have noted that the military conquests seem to be telescoped in these accounts. Instead of a continuing "war," as it were, the process historically seems to have spread over a much longer period, and to have resulted in Israelite and Canaanite pockets or "spheres of influence."

The book of Judges, on the other hand, is more down to earth. It concentrates on the steps which lay between promise and fulfillment, including the habitual infidelity to the Covenant, which brought in its wake defeat and subjugation.

At the time of the invasion, from 1250 B.C. onward, the Canaanites were a wealthy and highly civilized people. They lived in strongly fortified towns from which they could go out to work their farms. Politically, the country was swarming with tiny city-states.

Religion was a very sorry thing. The Canaanite gods were worshipped in the fertility cults largely for what the worshipper could get out of the religion. Sacrifices were looked upon as so many bribes to the god in order to get rain or a good harvest. In short, it might be called a religion of self-interest, in which ritual prostitution and human sacrifice had a part.

The investigations of the archeologists have shed a good deal of light on this period and offer many interesting confirmations of the authenticity of the accounts in Joshua and Judges. At the archeological tell of Hazor, for instance, in upper Galilee, the buried evidence proves that Canaanite idols had been shattered and burned. The site of Jericho is by far the oldest center of urban life in the world, many centuries before the time of Joshua. Do not worry about published statements concerning the archeologists' doubts about the dates of the walls of Jericho. The precise interpretation of the biblical account, as to how Jericho fell, is argued intensely. Probably the best reason why archeologists cannot identify the fallen walls of the Jericho of Joshua is that repeated flash floods moved and thus destroyed the evidence.

The Battle of Jericho

JOSHUA, Chapters 1 through 6:

The crossing of the Jordan recalls the crossing of the Reed Sea under Moses. It serves much the same purpose: to confirm Joshua as the divinely appointed leader of the people. It would seem that the miracle of the blockage of the upper waters was a providential act of God rather than a miracle in the strictest sense. We have at least two other examples of this drying up of the Jordan from relatively modern history as late as 1927. Both were perfectly natural in origin. The phenomenon seems due to the undermining of the banks of the river, so that from time to time a large section collapses into the stream and dams off the waters. But the finger of God is present in the timing of the event for the Israelites.

As for the battle of Jericho, the whole description has something of the flavor of a religious service, with the priests marching at the head of the army carrying the Ark of the Covenant and the sound of trumpets.

We suggest that you do not be concerned about some of the explanations of the fall of the walls, explanations that are highly farfetched at the best. One of the most inane of such attempts to "rescue" the biblical account and make it sound plausible is the claim that the feet of the people marching in unison set up harmonic vibrations in the ground, similar to a small earthquake, which caused the walls to topple. The fact is that Jericho fell, and that the Israelites attributed its fall to God's assistance. The biblical account, in line with the literary forms of its time, is not obliged to tell us of all the military means which the Israelites may have employed in order to attain their purpose.

JOSHUA, Chapters 23 and 24:

In these words of Joshua's farewell and death, you are reading a summary of the theme of the whole book. The aging general sums up his life's work and warns the people of the danger of contamination by contact with the idolatrous and licentious practices of their Canaanite neighbors. He recalls for the people all the love and care which God has lavished upon them since the time of Abraham, and calls for their loyalty to God's covenant.

JUDGES, Chapter 2:

This chapter is the introduction to the whole book, pointing up the religious interpretation of Jewish history. The leaders of the people were called "judges," as this was one of their chief duties, deciding disputes, but by no means their only one. The Hebrew word for judges might better be translated as "champions." The Judges were looked on as national heroes, but the fact is that they were the only symbols of law and order at a time when an established government did not exist.

JUDGES, Chapters 13 through 16:

These stories of Samson actually create a problem in one's mind if Samson were to be looked on as a devout religious hero. Devout he was not; irreligious and amoral and lusty, he was. For that matter, he was not an edifying figure in any sense. Why then was he included among the "judges" of the Israelites? Biblical scholarship has characterized him as a murderous bandit, a peasant of extraordinary strength, whose exploits have been even more magnified in folklore. The ultimate answer appears to be this: the stories of Samson were included here to show that through actions of a man like this, Yahweh helped His people survive against the Philistines.

King David

The disunited Israelites needed a strong central government and a powerful army in the face of repeated invasion by other wanderers and resistance from the earlier inhabitants. In the books of Samuel and Kings you will see how this strong government came to be, and at what price the people gained that security.

That price meant taxes, levies for armies, and on occasion, the existence of the despotism and corruption that was almost taken for granted in those days for kings to rule. The kings frequently forgot that they were merely representatives of the God of Israel, the only true ruler of Israel. They imitated the tyrannical policies of the neighboring petty lords. The traditions in the books of Samuel reflect these two sides of the story. The king, God's visible representative, is a sacred person, the one from whose line would one day come the looked-for Savior, Messiah, Anointed One. On the other hand, the king might also be a corrupt and vicious dictator, leading the people into idolatry and the eventual misery of exile far from the land of promise.

There are many ways of looking at King David. He was a military leader, a statesman, adventurer, and a poet. There is nothing of the plaster-cast image of St. King David. At times, his conduct reminds us of the most despotical of oriental potentates, rather than the saintly composer of religious songs. Yet his repentance has become the ideal of every conversion experience, embodied in a humility as deep as the earlier arrogant conceit which led to his sins.

READ: 1 Samuel, Chapters 13 through 28;
2 Samuel, Chapters 1 through 8; 11 and 12; 22.

The Political Situation

With the close of the era of the Judges, ancient Israel faced a situation similar in many ways to the situation faced by the founders of our own country. A loose federation was dangerously weak. The Israelites had been able to manage fairly well with this confederation when their only opponents were the petty princelings of Canaan. With the arrival of the Philistines and their lightning invasion of the coastal area, a situation rapidly developed which called for the most drastic measures.

The Israelite monarchy which resulted began with the accession of Saul in about 1020 B.C. The Philistines were natural enemies. They had different racial origins, language, religion, and civilization. In matters of warfare and culture they were superior, particularly in their expertise as mariners roving far and wide along the coasts of the Mediterranean. Their greatest hold over the Israelites was their jealously guarded secret of metal working and prowess as charioteers. Their own name was eventually given to the Holy Land, Palestine.

1 SAMUEL, Chapters 16-17:

In reading the life of David, you will notice a two-fold source making itself evident for some of the events in David's career. This is exemplified in the double account of David's introduction to public life, as in these chapters. It would appear that the historian selected from various traditions in composing his book and did not worry too much about harmonizing the various differences. You should note that the four books known as Samuel and Kings are really a single work. The division is purely artificial.

2 SAMUEL, Chapter 1:

David's lament for Saul and Jonathan is one of the masterpieces of ancient literature. The depth of human feeling it reflects does credit to the great heart of David.

2 SAMUEL, Chapter 5:

The capture of Jerusalem marks the high point of David's career. Jerusalem was the ideal spot for the new capital, as its geographic position made it a perfect and quasi-neutral anchor for uniting the northern and southern factions of the country. Jerusalem was also on the border of the Judean desert. Its strong fortification by David made it a bulwark against incursions from the brigands of the desert. For that matter, you must remember that David himself was for a time one of such brigands.

The bringing of the Ark of the Covenant to Jerusalem made the city not only the political but the religious heart of the country as well. As the centuries passed, Jerusalem became a sacred symbol for all that the Jews hoped for in the Messianic era.

2 SAMUEL, Chapter 11:

The account of Nathan's confrontation of David with his sin is one of the most dramatic in all literature. Too often, the emphasis is placed only on David's reaction; we should not forget the tremendous courage required in Nathan to stand up to this despot. The historical fact is that from this time on David is a changed man. His life becomes embroiled in a tangle of difficulties and sorrows which are to have terrible consequences for the future of his family and the whole of Israel. These political strains during the kingship of David already presage the open rebellion and division of the monarchy which were to flare up at the death of David's son, Solomon.

2 SAMUEL, Chapter 22:

This hymn of thanksgiving placed here by one of the editors of the Old Testament is identical with Psalm 18; it reflects the ancient tradition that David was one of the chief authors of the psalms. It gives not only some idea of the poetical gifts of its author, but is practically a character portrait of the man himself.

The Prophets

At this stage in our progression through the Old Testament, we must see in some detail how the biblical prophets fit into the biblical picture. If you expanded your reading in the books of Kings, you must have noticed the space devoted to the prophets Elijah and Elisha. In the story of David, it is the prophet Nathan who rebukes the king for his murder and his adultery.

But the prophets are a much larger and, in fact, a much more complex group than these three representatives. In fact, the prophets differ in their temperaments and outlooks among themselves as much as prophetical writings differ from the historical and wisdom literature in the Bible.

In an effort to catalogue these widely divergent groups, various attempts have been made in the past to classify them. They have been called "Major" and "Minor" prophets, more or less depending on the amount of written material we have concerning them. Isaiah, Jeremiah, Exechiel, and Daniel are the Major Prophets. The Minor Prophets are the twelve short writings of men such as Hosea and Amos—"minor" only because these writings are short. Jonah, too, is included among the Minor Prophets, although (as we shall see in our section on Wisdom Literature) the book of Jonah is not written by Jonah but rather is about Jonah.

Elijah, Elisha, and Nathan would be classified by some as "non-writing" prophets. But this adjective, too, is practically a misnomer. No prophet seems to have actually written his sermons. Instead, his disciples listened to what he said, transmitted through long and faithful tradition, and eventually someone set this tradition down in writing. You should particularly note the lack of order that generally exists among the prophets. This is due to the fact of the tradition. The tradition merely passed on the collected sayings of the great man, and did not especially care about the time or the place or the relative order in which the oracles were spoken.

Concerning the biblical prophets, the most important truth you should keep in mind is this: *The ultimate task of prophets and prophecy was not to foretell the future.* Their essential task was to call the people back to the observance of the will of God, to the Covenant. Even when the prophets did offer "signs" to vouch for the authenticity of their message, their pronouncements about the future were made in symbolic language and were often conditional.

In our own day the impression is widespread that the gift of prophecy is equivalent to a penchant for attacking and upsetting the current institutions and order of living. Few ideas could be farther removed from the truth. The legitimate biblical prophets did on occasion inveigh against contemporary customs and regime. Their rationale, however, was based on the iniquity of the regime, not on the fact that it was a regime wielding authority.

Some scholars have claimed that the biblical prophets were against organized religion. Again, that claim is false, for being incomplete. The prophets did on occasion protest against institutional religion, but only when institutional religion had degenerated into externals devoid of internal meaning and spirit, and therefore full hypocrisy and self-glorifying pride.

Social Reform and the Prophet Amos

The Israelite monarchy of the three kings of Saul, David, and Solomon lasted from about 1020 B.C. to 931 B.C. At the death of Solomon in 931, the tensions and jealousies within the monarchy broke loose, partly as a result of the oppressive rule and wasteful opulence of Solomon. The ten tribes of the north broke away into the kingdom of Israel. The two tribes of the south existed as the kingdom of Juda. It is a historical question that is difficult to decide as to which of the two kingdoms deserted the Covenant more. Certainly, both kingdoms had their share of "bad" kings.

READ: AMOS, Chapter 3 through 6; Chapters 7 through 9.

Amos was a social reformer, but his opposition to the wealthy was not based upon their oppression of the poor alone. The oppression was merely a symptom of the corrosive pride and God-defying self-indulgence that was the root of the evils in both kingdoms.

A new enemy had risen to threaten the two kingdoms. The Assyrians, the most brutal of brutal conquers of their day, were in the midst of a rapid conquest of all the Middle East. Wherever they went, terror went before them as their strongest ally.

As for the state of religion in the north, the kings of the new Israel severed all religious ties with Juda as well. People were not permitted to go on pilgrimage to the Temple at Jerusalem. Native northern shrines to Yahweh were established at Bethel and at Dan. These places were located in the provinces we know later as Samaria and Galilee.

During these years of separation the northern kingdom grew very wealthy. Yet its rich grew richer at the expense of its poor who grew poorer, reduced to virtual slavery. Amos addressed himself to try to correct these abuses.

Amos, himself from the hamlet of Tekoa near Bethlehem in the south, was probably a migratory worker, a trimmer of trees and a drover.

He had the countryman's ability to speak his mind in plain language, and should be reckoned among the most influential of all biblical prophets. (Note in this regard how incorrect a connotation results from listing Amos as a "Minor" Prophet.)

AMOS, Chapter 3:

The term, "chosen people," had come in Amos' day to be a source of great pride and complacency for the Israelites. They felt that because God had chosen them through Abraham, He had to make good on His promises regardless of their conduct. The prophet gave a completely different meaning to that idea of being chosen by God. He touched on an important theme that will recur in later prophetic writings, even into the New Testament: the "remnant." Although God's people had been false to the covenant, a few would be spared and would be the beneficiaries of the promise.

Amos condemns the callous-hearted rich and their false piety. Harsh though his words may be, there is no vindictiveness here. Only as a hurt cry of rejected love, Amos speaks for God. God sees His people abandoning Him for the road that leads to death and destruction, and, despite His pleading, "they will not return."

AMOS, Chapter 5:

In this chapter is the passage (verses 8-24) magnificently portraying the grandeur of God and His limitless power and majesty. This is contrasted sharply with the rebellion of mankind and the consequent day of judgment. This day of judgment—the "day of the Lord"—was a popular idea among the people of Israel. It was to be their day of triumph over the pagans, the gentile nations. The prophet, however, painted a completely differing picture of this "day," in an eloquent plea for the paramount importance of interior religion. Pride and hypocrisy are the enemies of true religion, making it devoid of meaning.

Isaiah

The mention of the Book of Isaiah offers an accurately pertinent example of the fact that the name of a book does not necessarily indicate its author, and that a single book of the Bible might come (as does Isaiah) from widely different periods.

Biblical scholarship divides Isaiah into three definite parts from three separate periods. The first is called "Proto-Isaiah" (First Isaiah), attributed to the prophet we call Isaiah from the 700's B.C. The second section is called "Deutero-Isaiah" (Second Isaiah) and is dated from about the middle 500's B.C. The third section, called by some scholars "Trito-Isaiah," comes from some time later. The chapters in question are 1 through 39 for the earliest part; 40 through 55 for the second, and 56 through 66 for the third.

Isaiah is definitely an anthology. It has been called a collection of collections, and it fits well into the pattern which we mentioned earlier, whereby the words of the prophet came not by his own writing but by the reports from his hearers.

Why was all this material assembled into the one book? The answer seems to lie in the fact that its tradition or school of thought was thought to belong to that of the original prophet Isaiah. There is little or no attempt to set down the sermons and poems in any kind of strict chronological order. The editor (whoever it was who assembled all this material into one collection) did not even attempt to give his work a story thread upon which to hand the various selections.

READ: ISAIAH, Chapters 1 through 12—the call of the prophet, and the "Emmanuel" prophecies;

ISAIAH, Chapters 42 through 53: The Servant Songs

Remember as you read these selections that Isaiah is one of the most frequently quoted books in the New Testament, second only to the Psalms and references to the Pentateuch. It is also one of the most frequently used sources for phrases in the liturgy.

In Proto-Isaiah, the scene is the southern kingdom of Juda. The time is the middle 700's, B.C., when Isaiah is attempting to save the southern kingdom from receiving the same annihilation that would be visited on the north, Israel, in 721 B.C. Isaiah seems to have been a member of the nobility. For this reason he had easy access to the king and to high officials of the nation. He appears to have played the part of elder statesman throughout much of his career. He was a keen observer of his times, and his deep insight into the awesome holiness of God did not cause him to divorce himself from life. His life was a perfect wedding of the mystic we meet in Chapter 6 enraptured with a vision of God's majesty, and the politician discussing affairs of state with King Achaz in Chapter 7. Even on merely practical grounds, his policy of non-intervention and neutrality in the struggle for control of the ancient world raging between Assyria and Egypt may well have been the only course that could have saved the national integrity of Juda.

ISAIAH, Chapter 1:

Here you have (in verse 3) an excellent example of a biblical quotation used for centuries in an "applied" sense. This applied sense means that an interpretation is taken out of a biblical text which is not in the original text. Sometimes this is also called an "accommodated" sense. The text in question was long used with reference to Christmas: "The ox knows its owner, and the ass its master's crib," with the implication that an ox and an ass were present in the cave at Bethlehem when Jesus was born. Yet the original, true meaning of Isaiah in the 700's B.C. was something completely different. He meant that while animals return home to their master's shelter, Israel has deserted its God and does not return. In Pope Pius XII's encyclical on Holy Scripture *(Divino Afflante Spiritu)*, the Pope made it clear that it was not a mistake to use this accommodated sense with discretion. There was a proviso: One should not claim the accommodation to be the meaning of the original biblical words, even though one might claim the fittingness of the accommodation.

Isaiah has also been used for centuries as a kind of source-book for accommodated biblical texts applied to the sufferings of Jesus on the cross. Thus, in verse 6, "From the sole of the foot even to the head there is no soundness in (Him) it," the original reference speaks of the spiritual sickness of Juda, certainly with no reference to the future Jesus.

ISAIAH, Chapter 2:

Verse 4 is one of the many Isaian phrases that have become even secular by-words: "beating swords into plowshares," as a symbol of times of peace.

ISAIAH, Chapter 3:

Verses 18 through 24 are a pertinent example of incidental references which tell us of the styles of the times. In this instance, the coming woes of the haughty women of Juda are enumerated by detailing the exchange of their expensive wardrobes for the status of female slaves.

ISAIAH, Chapter 5:

This "vineyard chapter" can serve to introduce you to the comparison with the vineyard and God's people, as Jesus used it later in the New Testament. The power of the parables of the vineyard is more accurately understood when we see the New Testament parables against the background of this Isaian Old Testament chapter—certainly so well known to the contemporaries of Jesus.

ISAIAH, Chapter 6:

This is the famous chapter about the call of the prophet. Notice how it exemplifies the lack of order in Isaiah; disparate sayings of the prophet took up the first five chapters, although we would have expected this "official" vocation of Isaiah logically to begin the book instead.

This vision sets the tone of the whole of Isaiah's mission. He was to be the great prophet of God's holiness. In the Old Testament, the idea of holiness meant to be separated from whatever is base and impure. Applied to God, it signified His complete "apartness" and distinction from the things He created. God stands completely above and apart from His creation. Yet this is not the whole story. God's holiness is also active and makes demands upon mankind. God is also holy because He makes holy. God wishes His creation to share His holiness. In Isaiah, we meet the outlines of God's wish to share His holiness with His creation, that mankind might share in the divine life of God.

The vision takes place in the Temple. Up to this time the appearances of God to man had taken place almost exclusively in desert places. The picture which Isaiah paints is very similar to what one might have seen in the audience hall of some great Oriental potentate, with the monarch seated upon this throne.

Verses 8 through 13 reinforce the picture of the true prophetic vocation: again, not that of foretelling the future, but really meaning "one who speaks for another." The prophet was to speak to the king and to the people, in the name of God, and to be the national conscience. Sometimes in his role of public conscience it might be necessary to point out the future results of present conduct, but this was not always necessary or a primary feature of the prophet's work.

Verses 9 through 13 must not be understood as some sort of harsh predestination to reprobation of the humans who refuse to hear the word of God. The words recur as quoted, in the New Testament gospels. Actually, they are a sort of "Semitism," a Hebraic way of speaking, whereby man's resulting action is pictured as if God had determined it in advance, independently of man's free will. We might put the same idea in different words: Whereas our way of thinking would think of man's refusal to hear God through Isaiah as a *result,* the biblical way of thinking looks on this refusal as if it were God's all-powerful *purpose.* The reason is that God does, after all, control everything as Creator.

ISAIAH, Chapter 7 through 11.

These are called "the Emmanuel prophecies" from the Hebrew phrase,

"God with us" (Emmanuel). In context, they are references to contemporaneous history. Later centuries saw in them (as did the Gospels) references to the life and actions of the divine Savior, Jesus Christ.

Few if any texts in the Bible have been quoted so often as "The Virgin will conceive" of verse 14. Few texts have been so hotly disputed as to their original meaning. This is the background in history:

Throughout this period (742-725 B.C.) Assyria was an evergrowing menace to the independence of the petty princelings of Palestine and Syria. Having secured the unreliable backing of Egypt, which was a mere shell of the powerful Egyptian empire of an earlier day, three of these little kingdoms formed a coalition under the leadership of the city of Damascus. King Achaz of Juda refused to join the league. This was disastrous to the plans of the league because Juda was the overland link with Egypt in case they should need military assistance from the south. The only thing for the coalition to do was to march on Juda, to dethrone Achaz, and to put one of their own men in his place. At the time of this meeting of Achaz and Isaiah, word had reached the capital that the coalition was marching against it. It was probably on a tour of inspection of the fortifications that the monarch met the prophet. (Cf. 2 Kings 16, 1-20)

ISAIAH, Chapter 7:

Few passages are as well known and have been argued over as much as Isaiah 7:14. One of the chief reasons for this predilection is the use made of these words in Matthew 1, 22, where it appears to be understood as predicting the virgin birth of Jesus. We must acknowledge that the word which Matthew translates as *parthenos* in the Greek New Testament has a more specific meaning as "virgin" than does the *almah* of Isaiah's Hebrew, which connotes a young girl not yet married. Scholars argue whether Matthew refers primarily to the virgin birth of Jesus or to the Davidic origin of Jesus as Messiah.

The undeniable fact is that the New Testament draws deeper meaning from the words of Isaiah; but in the times of Isaiah, the meaning at the moment seems to have been the prediction that the enemies of Juda will be destroyed in the time that the "Emmanuel" child of the *almah* will need to reach his use of reason.

Who is the "Emmanuel"? The name in Hebrew means, "God with us." Various explanations exist, certainly not all in agreement. Some have claimed that Emmanuel refers to a son to be born to Achaz himself, others to Isaiah's son, but the reference to the son of Achaz, Hezekiah, seems most likely. Centuries later, Matthew in the New Testament would discern a strikingly pertinent application to Jesus Christ as "God with us." In view of the God-willed obscurity of the incarnation of Jesus, it would be extremely difficult to hold the opinion that Isaiah somehow or other was aware that his words spoke of Jesus Christ, seven hundred years and more before the birth of Jesus. At the time of Matthew, however, the case was different.

ISAIAH, Chapters 42 to 53:

These poems are called "The Servant Songs" because they are about a person identified as God's suffering servant.

SONG #1: Isaiah, Chapter 42, 1-4: God presents His servant to the heavenly court. The servant is to be the patient teacher of the true faith of all mankind.

SONG #2: Isaiah, Chapter 49, 1-6: Here the servant speaks out to the whole world. It is interesting to note that the servant's mission is first to the lost sheep of the House of Israel, but apparently (49, 6) he will leave this work incomplete and turn to the gentile nations.

SONG #3: Isaiah, Chapter 50, 4-9: This might well be called the servant's Gethsemani. Yet even in the face of suffering he does not lose confidence in the fulfillment of his mission.

SONG #4: Isaiah, 52, 13 to 53, 12: This is by common consent the most important of these songs. It forms a striking portrait of the "Man of Sorrow."

Who is this suffering servant? The section occurs in Deutero-Isaiah, which has been described as biblical scholars as one of the most brilliant parts of the Old Testament; its author, they say, must have been a literary genius. The interpretation given to the identity of the suffering servant is widely variant. Jewish scholars have come to identify the servant either with the messiah (savior) to come, or with the nation itself, or with the faithful "remnant" few in every generation.

Christian scholars were unanimous in identifying the servant with Christ until the beginning of the eighteenth century. Today they are divided upon whether it refers only to Christ, but many would probably agree that the songs have definite messianic features. Jesus chose to fulfill this ideal of scripture in His own person. The Church has for centuries accepted (at least in the accommodated sense) these passages as a remarkable prophetic interpretation of the mission, passion, and death of Jesus.

Jeremiah

Jeremiah was born about the middle of the 600's B.C., and died time after the Babylonians took Jerusalem in 587 B.C. His book is longest book in the Bible, and his accounts are the most informati among the Old Testament prophets as to the identity and personal feelings of their author. In fact, Jeremiah's "confessions" have a special teaching value in showing how a faithful servant of God can go forward and accomplish a most distasteful God-given task, despite his inward conviction of unworthiness, not to mention his shyness as well.

Before doing some of the readings, note that Jeremiah is one of the two great prophets of the Exile, although he did not go to Babylon as did Ezechiel. He had long realized before Jewish royal officials saw the fact, that Babylon would soon conquer Jerusalem. He also saw in this a punishment of God for Juda's unfaithfulness to Yahweh, yet as always, this punishment was a form of God's mercy to save His people.

Note, too, how complex is the literary organization of Jeremiah. His sayings have been put together by an editor or editors in a way that does not classify the materials according to identical topics or similar occasions or even with the same kind of literary form. In fact, the unhomogeneous collection of Jeremiah is a pertinent example of one of our greatest modern difficulties in reading the prophets: you must constantly keep in mind that the scene may have shifted, the audience may have been changed, the topic may have become wholly different, and the time abruptly advanced, all with no "stage directions" to tell you of this fact.

Among the biographical details found in Jeremiah, there is one instance that illustrates for us how a prophet's collection may have come into existence. In 605 Jeremiah had assembled all his discourses up to that date in a document (really a "scroll) which his secretary Baruch was to read to the people in the Temple. The king Jehoiakim was highly incensed by the contents of this scroll, and destroyed it when it was read to him; he felt it was encouraging surrender to Babylon. Thereupon, Jeremiah says, the prophet dictated to Baruch another scroll which contained not only the original but added more oracles as well.

The autobiographical details from Jeremiah's life are generally held to exist in chapters 1-25; the biographical details (probably composed by Baruch) in chapters 26-45.

READ: selections as you find them interesting from the above chapters. Note in particular the following special sections which are classified as part of Jeremiah's "confessions":

Ezechiel

Ezechiel was the son of a Jerusalem priest named Buzi. His father had been priest before him serving in the Temple. Ezechiel was an ardent patriot and of all the prophets, the most extraordinary in his recounting of mystical experiences.

This combination of mystic and man of affairs is a striking one. Because of his visions, psychic experiences, and acted-out experiences, Ezechiel may seem a very strange and bizarre figure to you. In this reaction you would be far from alone. Even Jewish rabbis many centuries ago felt that Ezechiel was so difficult to understand that no Jew was to be permitted to read the book until reaching thirty years of age.

Most of the book of Ezechiel is considered by scholars to be the work of the man to whom it is attributed. However, as is so often the case in other biblical books as well, large portions seem to have come from other sources but were united into this one book under the one name and title.

Ezechiel lived and prophesied among the Jewish exiles in Babylon. He was the prophet of the displaced exiles from 597 to 538 B.C. His task was to urge the tiny remnant in Babylon not to lose hope that the Lord would not forget them in their distress. Note that chapters 1 to 35 are markedly pessimistic, while chapters 36 to 48 are joyously optimistic.

READINGS: select according to your available time and interest:

"The Throne of God"—Ez. 1.
"The Prophet's Call"—Ez. 2 and 3.
"The Allegory of the Faithless Wife"—Ez. 16
"Punishment and Pardon"—Ez. 18.
"The Death of Ezechiel's Wife"—Ez. 24, 15-27.
"Hope and Consolation"—Ez. 33 and 34.
"The Restoration"—Ez. 36, 16 to 37, 14.
(Chapters 25-32 are considered worthwhile for their beauty.)

EZECHIEL, Chapter 1:

This is the centuries-famous description of God's throne, in exceptionally symbolic language. When reading it, do not be misled into thinking it is self-contradictory, as if it were some sort of treatise on mechanics when the wheels on God's chariot are at four corners, are at right angles, and simultaneously go in all directions at once. The symbolism is that God is above and beyond all description, that God is everywhere and all-powerful.

It is here in this chapter that you will find mentioned (not for the first time in the Bible, nor for the last) the characteristics of the "cherubim" who supported God's throne. The concept of beings borrowed from pagan mythology but purified to serve at the throne of God became eventually our modern concept of angelic spirits serving God. But the four attributes occur here most clearly: the face of the man signifying intelligence; the body of the lion signifying aggressive bravery; the hooves of the ox signifying strength; and the wings of the bird or eagle signifying the immediacy of God's presence everywhere.

Looked at in the light of this constant symbolism of the transcendence of God and God's unapproachability by man, Ezechiel's vision of the throne of God can teach symbolically a deep reverence for the majesty of the all-good and the wholly other: Yahweh.

HIGHPOINTS OF THESE SELECTIONS:

"The soul that sins, it shall die." EZ. 18, 1-4.

Ezechiel is the first of the prophets to bring out fully that God is interested in the individual person. The ancient Israelites were so strongly aware of God's concern for the nation that in practice they seemed to be practically unaware of individual responsibility and direct personal relations of a man and a woman to their God. Ezechiel vividly brought out the idea of individual retribution contrasted to group retribution by quoting the proverb, "The fathers have eaten sour grapes, and the children's teeth are set on edge." The truth of the situation is that all of us humans are in fact dependent on the actions not only of our ancestors but on the actions of our fellow humans who make decisions affecting our welfare. However, individual responsibility and individual morality cannot be affected by the actions of anyone except the individual.

"The desire of thine eyes." EZ. 24, 15-17.

Some commentators think that the death of Ezechiel's wife so stunned him that he was unable to give vent to his grief in the usual wailing and lamentation. God forewarned him of the personal tragedy that he might understand another significance beyond that of his personal loss. Other scholars interpret this passage somewhat differently. They believe that the whole story is a symbolic description of the grief of the exiles at the fall of Jerusalem.

"I have set you a watchman for my people." EZ. 34, 16-31.

The fall of Jerusalem is the turning point in Ezechiel's career. To mark this transition from prophet of doom to prophet of hope, the call and mission of Ezechiel are stated once again.

AFTER THE PROPHETS: Ezra and Nehemiah. (Chronicles)

READ: Nehemiah, Ch. 2, 4, 6.
Ezra, Ch. 9, 10.

These are short selections, to give some indication of what was happening in Jewish history after the exiles returned to Jerusalem from Babylon. For our present interests, it is quite important to note that scholars consider the author of Ezra and Nehemiah to be the same person who composed the two books of Chronicles. While we have not suggested extensive readings in Chronicles, since this might take our overview too far afield and into too much detail, you might be interested to sample selections of Chronicles in the light of their authorship by the same man who wrote Ezra and Nehemiah. You should remember, however, that Chronicles was not intended to be a history in the same sense as other historical books of the Bible. Sometimes it has been almost a source of scandal to Bible readers to hear that Chronicles suppresses, as it were, some of the scandalous and less edifying events described in other parts of the Bible. The reason is that the author of Chronicles wrote his work not so much to show history as it was, but rather as it ideally might have been and should have been. Understood in this sense, his production is anything but deceptive. Understanding it in the full meaning of a literary form, it expressed "the meaning which its author intended to convey." It should not be read outside that context.

Ezra, Nehemiah, and Chronicles all are ascribed as most probably originating in the 400's B.C., even though their contents refer to centuries earlier. Ezra and Nehemiah particularly describe the return of the exiles to Jerusalem and the task of rebuilding the city and restoring the meaning of Judaism.

We should note that the "diaspora" or spread of Jews throughout the world dated from the time of the exile to Babylon. Ever since that time, Jews established settlements in various cities where they banded together in a group attempt to retain their ancestral customs and their ancestral religion.

It was in the late 500's B.C., some time after 537 that the exiles were permitted to return to Jerusalem under the benign regime of the Persians.

The Persians had conquered the erstwhile conquerors, the Babylonians, and the difference in policy was that the Persian emperors considered it better for their empire to cooperate in the religious customs of their subjects as much as possible, thus making the task so much easier of controlling captive peoples.

Throughout the fifty years of the exile, Jerusalem was largely uninhabited and in ruins. The fields were mostly untilled, and the survivors had been greeted with apathy and even open hostility by those who had remained in Palestine during the exile. These last were a mixture of Jews and pagans with whom they had intermarried. This was hardly the glorious restoration the exiles had dreamed of in Babylon, and many gave in to despair.

Nehemiah, the civil governor, labored valiantly to rebuild the walls of the city and to establish a toehold for Israel in the former homeland. Ezra the priest some years later labored with equal dedication to build a "Wall of Law" around the remnant of Israel. Behind this "Wall of Law," the Jews were to live a self-contained life. Political power was gone. But some of the leaders of the people, Ezra and Nehemiah in particular, were determined at all cost to keep the nation faithful to its spiritual mission of preserving the flame of faith until the day of the Lord arrived.

It is with the return from exile that we first encounter the word "Jew." This new word makes a new stage. It was a time of preserving the faith handed down from the fathers, and new growth towards a more spiritual faith. It was to this period that the customs and forms of worship familiar in New Testament times trace their origin.

At this time, the "scribes," mostly laymen devoted to the study and application of the law, began their rise to prominence. We should refrain, however, from considering the scribes of this period as identical to the scribes of the time of Jesus; much development still was to occur. Two new religious institutions, the council of elders or *Sanhedrin,* largely replacing the king as governing body, and the various local *synagogues,* increasingly the center of religious teaching and worship, also date from this period.

Highpoints of these selections:

"I fixed him a time" Neh. 2, 6.

Nehemiah was to exercise his office of Jewish governor for some twelve years. It is interesting to note that Nehemiah carefully avoids any mention of building fortifications other than the small temple guard-post, as this would be sure to arouse the suspicions of an absent monarch. That the Persian emperor permitted the Jews to return to Palestine at all is a striking example of the more liberal policies pursued by these monarchs in contrast to the crushing despotism of the Assyrians and Babylonians.

"Sanballat and Tobiah" Neh. 2, 10.

These two men were to head the opposition. Sanballat was the governor of Samaria, while Tobiah was the head of the wealthy Tobiad family. Both these men had a vested interest in seeing that no permanent restoration of Jews in Palestine came about.

"The Samaritans" Neh. 2, 20.

Compare this verse with Ezra, 4, 1-6. The abhorrence which the strict and zealous leader of the new Israel felt for the surrounding people can be readily imagined. The Samaritans' offer to help was in particular brusquely rebuffed. The Samaritans were the people whom the Assyrians had planted in northern Palestine to replace the deported Israelites (about 721 B.C.). They had intermarried there with the remaining Israelites and adopted various observances of the Hebrew religion, mixing it with their native paganism. This refusal of help in rebuilding Jerusalem and the Temple was one of the origins of the feud between Jew and Samaritan lasting up to the time of Jesus. Scholars caution us against ascribing one or other cause to this enmity. The genuine sources of the antagonism seem to have been multifold and deep-rooted.

"A False Friend" Neh. 6, 10.

The walls were now finished, and there was little danger of a successful military attack from without. Sanballat and Tobiah now embarked on a series of plots and intrigues. The particular scheme narrated here was an attempt to discredit Nehemiah in the eyes of the people. No layman was permitted to enter the inner sanctuary of the Temple.

"The Question of Marriage with non-Jews" Ez. 9, 1-15.

Throughout the history of the Jews, this had been a constant problem. You might be interested in picking up other pronouncements on this point: Exodus, 34, 15-16; Deuteronomy, 7, 1-5; 1 Kings 11, 1-13, which clearly show what a great danger to the faith intermarriage with the neighboring pagans had always been—and remained.

"A Stern Solution" Ez. 10.

The harsh measures adopted were called for by the grave state of emergency then existing. The feeble band of returned exiles and lukewarm people of the land were extremely vulnerable to external influences. Ezra felt that if intermarriage continued, his little band of Jews would disappear into the melting pot of the Middle East.

WISDOM LITERATURE

It is a very difficult task to try to classify the various books of the Bible into air-tight, neatly defined divisions. To begin with, they were not written to fit any such classification. Only as the years progressed did some diversification become noticed as such. In general, we have been following to this point a broad outline of historical and prophetical works. Now, we are including the remaining readings in the genre of "Wisdom Literature." In the strictest sense of Wisdom Literature, some of the titles to be discussed might come closer to our modern version of a historical novel; but if we were to think of them as attempting to teach a lesson, particularly a lesson in moral living, then we would be approaching the biblical concept of "wisdom."

Actually, it would be very erroneous to think that the Bible gives information on all matters under the sun. Its "wisdom" goes into various directions of popular interest and popular value. These areas have been defined thus:

a) *A consideration of the problem of evil, suffering, and death.* The problem has bedevilled the human race to the origins of written history. Why do good people suffer? Why is there no direct proportion between doing good, avoiding evil, and enjoying happiness on this earth? Why do the evil so often (yet not always) enjoy prosperity? Why do innocent children suffer?

b) *Proverbial wisdom.* The biblical books of proverb collections are not essentially different from other such collections of their time. The topics are generally the same, namely, the use of wealth, friends, family, power, hospitality; and the troubles arising from the misuse of alcoholic drink, wanton women, betrayed confidences, and loaned or borrowed money.

c) *Advice for young men, particularly at court.* This is a sort of special subdivision of proverbial wisdom, adapted for the culture of its time. In our own day it might be entitled, "How to get along in the world as a successful person."

The Psalms

The book of Psalms is our first example of wisdom literature, even though in its own way it is so utterly unique and includes psalms that are historic or prophetic in their content. If there were no other book in the

Bible in existence, it has been said, the existence of the Psalms alone would be enough to call attention to religious poetry that is unsurpassed, perhaps even unequalled in the literature of the world.

The word "psalm" has its roots in the sense of playing on a stringed instrument. Theoretically speaking, the psalms were made to be sung to the accompaniment of such an instrument. In practice, however, the fact that they are merely read detracts in no way from their quality of being religious hymns.

The psalms were not written at one time nor by one author. Many of them are attributed to King David, with great probability. Some of them seem to have been written after the Babylonian exile, but an apodictic claim to know the age of each psalm is practically impossible to defend. The one quality that all scholars can agree on is that the present collection of psalms comes from several earlier collections, which evidently were in a state of flux throughout the centuries. You yourself do not have to be an erudite biblical scholar to note that some psalms are composed of two or more separate sections which could be separately listed; or else some psalms that succeed each other could be joined with no violation to the continuity of their theme.

The diversity of content of the psalms has led to various schemes of classification. What we suggest here summarizes the conclusions that seem generally accepted:

1) *Royal psalms.* This refers to songs for enthroning the king, but with the advance of time the "kingly" psalms began to be looked on as references to the messianic or "savior" king.

2) *Hymns.* It is particularly in this area that you will find for yourself some of the most sublime and selfless prayers of adoration. The concept of praising God for His own goodness and majesty, independently of our own needs, recurs again and again.

3) *Lamentation psalms, both individual and collective.* The repeated cries of the psalmist author for help have sometimes been interpreted as prayers from the group rather than from the individual; but you will be able to see in some cases for yourself that a "collective" interpretation can hardly fit prayers evidently coming deep from personal need. The psalms have sometimes been given superficial criticism for too much pessimism, too much "whining" about problems and troubles. The answer to this untrue objection can be found when any individual himself or herself is in deep misery. Only someone suffering acutely can fully appreciate the comfort of these calls to God for help.

4) *Thanksgiving psalms.* Like the songs of adoration, the psalms of gratitude are excellent models of prayers of thanksgiving in our own lives.

5) *Prophetic psalms, and Wisdom psalms.* These imitate contents of prophetic and wisdom books respectively.

6) *Recitations of history.* These are usually surveys of the history of the Jews, with particular emphasis on faithfulness to the God of Israel for His protection and mercy.

Notice, however, that these divisions are not completely exclusive, despite the pronouncements of biblical scholars on them. One and the same psalm can move from one mood or outlook to another, again defying a single classification.

Do not be surprised in your reading to find some psalms repeated; this re-occurrence is one more proof that our present psalter is only the final step in what must have been repeated collections.

The numbers of the psalms historically have been a source of great confusion. There is little hope that this confusion will ever disappear unless the present trend to list only the Hebrew numbering in contemporary biblical editions continues. The confusion arose from the fact that the Septuagint Greek, Latin Vulgate, and English translations derived from these sources tabulated the psalms differently from 9 to 148. The easiest way to recall the difference is to expect that the Hebrew numberings are one more than the Greek, starting with Psalm 10 and ending with psalm 146. The difference arose because one system joined certain psalms which the other system separated. As should be obvious, absolutely no religious doctrine or policy is involved, even though the unfortunate captions of "Protestant" and "Catholic" became attached to the Hebrew and Greek respectively.

Do not expect to find either rhyme or rhythm in your English translation of the psalms. Scholars differ whether the original Hebrew possesses rhyme or rhythm; such does not seem to be the property of Hebrew poetry. The poetic element rather lies in the lyric thought. It is also expressed formally in types of parallelism such as these:

1) *Synonymous parallelism.* Here one sentence or group of words or group of sentences repeats the same idea in different words.

2) *Antithetical parallelism.* Here the psalm presents a sharp contrast to the original thought by way of denying the opposite, for emphasis.

3) *Synthetic or constructive parallelism.* While this is listed by scholars as a separate category, one must candidly look on it more as a catch-all designation, to include developments of thought which cannot be otherwise

classified. Usually what happens is this: The psalm enuntiates one idea, then repeats the idea with an addition, then tacks on another addition, and so forth.

Do not take the "titles" or alleged descriptions introducing the psalms as completely historically valid. They appear to have been written long years if not centuries after the psalms themselves. In some cases they refer to the tune to be sung, in some cases they refer to instruments, in some cases they are Hebrew words whose meaning is unknown.

READING: In all other instances of biblical books, we have suggested certain samplings. In the case of the psalms, we suggest that you read *all* of the psalms, if possible; or at the minimum, that you page through the collection and read those which strike your fancy. In any event, it should be a richly rewarding experience.

Psalms for Special Comment: (Numbering is according to the Hebrew system)

PSALM 8: Note the description of the majesty of God, condescending to give mankind such special dignity.

PSALM 14: "The fool says in his heart, 'There is no God,' " refers to the biblical atheist. Yet you should note that theoretical atheism was practically unknown, i.e. that a man would argue against the existence of God. Instead, the "atheist" was one who lived practically *as if* God did not exist.

PSALM 22: The opening words, "My God, my God, why have you forsaken me?" are already the answer to the mistaken impression that Jesus Christ was supposedly in despair on the cross when he uttered this cry. The fact is that Jesus was praying this psalm, and as you read it through to the end, you will note that it ends on a prayer of complete hope in God's loving care.

PSALM 23: This is perhaps the best known of all psalms, "The Lord is my shepherd."

PSALM 34, verse 11: "Come, children, listen to me, I will teach you the fear of the Lord." This common phrase in the Wisdom literature, "the fear of the Lord," does not mean a terrifying dread of a tyrannical creator; instead, it is a loving reverence for God, as the context here and elsewhere amply demonstrates.

PSALM 51: This is the centuries-famous prayer for forgiveness called in Latin, the *Miserere*. It is ascribed to David, particularly as David's contrition after his sins of adultery and murder.

PSALM 84: Here you read the love of the pious Jew for the Temple as the special dwelling-place of God on earth.

PSALM 86: Some individuals would vote, in the difficult question of the most beautiful of all psalms, for this prayer of trust as that most beautiful. Its Verse 15 echoes a recurring tribute to God in other biblical writings: God is gracious and merciful, slow to anger and abounding in steadfast love and faithfulness.

PSALM 103: A close competitor for the title of "most beautiful" is this call to praise the goodness and mercy of the Lord, again repeating the tribute from Psalm 86:15.

PSALMS 111 through 117 are songs of praise, and for that reason are listed as part of the "Hallel"—"Praise the Lord"—group.

PSALM 118, Verse 25, has the distinction of having given us our word "hosanna," as a cry of joy. Actually, the word in Hebrew in the psalm says, "Make us safe," or "Save us." Its connection with joy came about because at the time this psalm was being sung in the Temple, the people would wave branches or sheaves of wheat at this point.

PSALM 119 is the longest of all the psalms, and represents an unbroken praise of God's law. Notice the many synonyms that recur for this law of God—path, commandments, statutes, ordinances, and the like.

PSALMS 120 through 135 are considered "songs of ascent," particularly suited for pilgrims to sing as they "ascended"—climbed the heights—on their way to reach Jerusalem.

PSALM 136 is the prototype of the modern litany kind of prayer, with its repeated anthem, "for his mercy (steadfast love) endures forever."

PSALM 137, referring to the Babylonian exile, might appear very bloodthirsty to us for its wish to "dash the little ones (of Babylon) against the rock." We can explain it only as an impassioned prayer, or as a cry for vengeance from an unenlightened conscience, or as an exaggerated literary expression.

PSALMS 146 through 150: The psalter ends with a final repeated call to praise the Lord in selfless adoration.

The Book of Job

It should be something of a thrill to realize that while you are reading the book of Job, you have before you one of the world's greatest masterpieces of literature. Job represents the high point of all biblical attempts to explain the problem of suffering. Yet even this single collection exemplifies the difficulties of finding an answer. The book of Job in a sense does not give the final answer, since it makes it clear that mankind is not capable of understanding God's plans. Depending on which portions of the book you select, you could even make a case for the opinion that Job offers contradictory explanations for its problem.

What precisely is the "problem of suffering"? It is not thoroughly accurate to word it in such a way as to say that the good always go unrewarded and that the evil always go unpunished. It seems closer to the truth to say that there does not seem to exist a proper and consistent proportion between some compensation for doing good contrasted to retribution for doing evil. Add to that the questions why innocent children have to suffer, and why so much suffering seems so meaningless coupled with the final inescapable end of death, and you have the correct picture.

Like practically all other books in the Bible, Job does not come from one author at one period of time. The oldest portions seem to be the opening portions (1, 1 to 2, 13, and 42, 7 to 42, 17) that reflect an ancient folktale of a "patient" Job, who suffered much innocently, and in the end received heaping rewards in this life. This attitude, that good people *are* rewarded in this life sufficiently, appears elsewhere in biblical writings, particularly in certain psalms. Scholarly studies believe that this "primitive" Job goes back to 1000 B.C.

You yourself can easily notice how the style changes with Chapter 3. There, an anonymous poet from some time after the Exile (perhaps in the 400's B.C.) took a different tack. He presented the picture of an "impatient" Job, the reality of one whose sufferings break his spirit and make him cry out in mental agony. This unit of Job consists of a "debate" between Job and three so-called friends, each of whom presents his position on three occasions, allowing Job a rebuttal each time. The friends' outlook summarizes another ancient belief appearing in biblical pages: If you are suffering greatly, that must mean that you are being punished for your great sins. Job, however, while admitting his imperfections, steadfastly maintains that his sinfulness is not so great as to bring about such dreadful misfortunes.

A later poet, again anonymous and at an unknown date, added still another outlook: Suffering is good for us, because it builds character, and without the need to suffer, we would never grow in strength. Job's answer to this is that his sufferings are far too great to be justified by an appeal to strengthening his character.

There you see how the skillful editor of this collection united the varying and sometimes contradictory solutions humankind has proposed in its history. In fact, the third author mentioned above used a further dramatic ploy to put the "strength of character" argument into the mouth of Elihu, the young man, who tells his elders from the depths of his inexperience that they do not know what they are talking about!

READ: JOB, 1 through 6; 19; 32; 38; 42, 7 to the end.

SOME SPECIAL COMMENTS:

The ancient Hebrews seem to have had very little knowledge of man's fate after death. It is only in the very last books of the Old Testament written shortly before the time of Christ (e.g. 2 Maccabees and Book of Wisdom) that we find here and there a clearer picture of mankind's eternal destiny. To the authors of Job, the only thing which awaited man at death was *Sheol.* It was a place of living a shadowy existence that was hardly an existence. It was not thought to be a place of great happiness at all, except for the fact that the good people did not suffer in the way that the evil did. Hence, rewards from God consisted in rewards of life on this earth: health, long life, many children, domestic peace. We moderns have great difficulty in comprehending this attitude toward the hereafter, but we must remember that there is a development in biblical belief on this topic as on so many others. Only later did the full acceptance of a heaven and a hell appear.

JOB, 19, 25-26:

These verses are among the most famous anywhere in the bible. You may have heard them in the aria, "I Know that My Redeemer Liveth," from Handel's *Messiah.* The question is precisely this: Does Job at this time profess belief in the resurrection of the body when he appears to say that he knows his "Redeemer" lives, and after Job's "skin" has been destroyed, "in his flesh" and "with his eyes" Job will see God?

The main answer is that Job could not possibly have possessed so rich a belief in the afterlife, much less a belief in the resurrection of the physical body. If Job had known such a thing, then the whole problem of the book of Job would have disappeared, in the sense that suffering and evil are not explained here in this life, but since there is an afterlife, everything is made right there.

How, then, did the impression exist from words that seem quite explicit, that Job does profess faith in the resurrection of the body? The answer lies in the fact that these verses are hopelessly corrupt in their original Hebrew reading. It has even been suggested that the text was deliberately changed by some scribes who at a later date wished to take sides against the growing Jewish belief in the resurrection of the body. It is certain that no one today knows what the original Hebrew reading must have been.

When St. Jerome, the learned genius of the 400's A.D., translated this text into the Latin Vulgate version, Jerome reconstructed it (as every translator must attempt to reconstruct it) into words that would indicate an explicit belief of Job in the resurrection of the body. Modern scholarship is unanimous in saying this reads too much into the controverted text. The word for "redeemer" or "vindicator" is rather a reference to the next of kin who had the obligation to avenge an injustice done to a close relative.

Does this controversy as to the meaning of Job's words damage in any way the testimony for the Christian belief in the resurrection of the body? Not at all, since that belief comes from other biblical sources, including the words of Jesus. The point at issue concerns *only* this one text in the Old Testament book of Job.

The example highlights the relative rarity of such corrupt texts in the bible. As we mentioned in the Introduction to these pages, instances of doubtful readings on an important doctrinal topic are so few that for practical purposes they can be overlooked.

Proverbs and Ben Sira (Ecclesiasticus)

READ: sample selections at your convenience and interest throughout the Book of Proverbs and the book of Sirach (also called Ben Sira—Son of Sirach—and Ecclesiasticus). Random sampling done frequently will give you a better idea of the contents of these two books than very lengthy readings of one portion alone.

The Book of Proverbs and Ecclesiasticus are quite parallel in their contents, and are good examples of wisdom literature in the Bible. Our comments here are for the purpose of putting these two works in proper perspective, so that they can be better understood and appreciated.

First of all, note that these two are equally inspired parts of the Bible together with the historical or prophetical works which might seem more "religious" and devotional because of their contents. The norm of inspiration remains, here as elsewhere, the action of God's cooperation with human authors; if an individual looks for inspiring, edifying, or explicitly devout sections to "prove" that God is co-author, that person will be disappointed. These two wisdom books are among the most earthy of all biblical writings. They are concerned about conduct in everyday life, and the subjects they discuss run the gamut of such everyday life in the Israel of their day.

The Book of Proverbs is a compilation of at least seven collections of proverbs, some of which might go back to 900 B.C. and the court of Solomon; the latest of them would definitely be after the Exile, six hundred or more years later.

The Book of Ecclesiasticus gets its name from a historical subtitle, "as read in the churches." It is one of the latest books in the Old Testament. Its relatively late composition as well as its Greek introduction may well have been the reasons why Hebrew sages considered it outside the original biblical canon. It is one of the deutero-canonical biblical books concerning which doubt existed for a time as to their inspiration and canonicity (these books, as explained in the Introduction, are also called the apocrypha). Its names "ben Sirach" or "Son of Sirach" come from the fact that its author is "Jesus, son of Eleazer, son of Sirach."

A few lines previously, we mentioned that the proverbial contents of the Bible, as exemplified here, are among the most earthy of all biblical books. Notice this list of topics considered in these proverbs, particularly the comments on misogyny, negative attitudes toward women:

1. *WOMEN.* A great deal of publicity has appeared against the supposed woman-hating attitudes of these biblical books, allegedly picturing women in a bad light. In fairness and in justice, the references to women should be analyzed objectively. Certainly, Ecclesiasticus 25 closes with anything but praise for the spiteful, garrulous woman whose face is "grim as any bear's," causing her husband to heave bitter sighs when he goes out for dinner with his neighbors; the section closes with the comment that sin began with a woman, and thanks to her we all die!

Other comments, however, appear to be more justified in the condemnation of the seductive adulterous woman who lures gullible young men to their destruction; such are the repeated warnings to the young men to avoid all dealings with such persons.

In the opposite direction, good women receive praise as well. Chapter 26 of Ecclesiasticus goes to great lengths first to condemn the bad wife, but then to exalt the beauty of character and of body of the good wife. Almost all of Chapter 31 of Proverbs is made up of an alphabetic poem on the virtues of the perfect wife of those days. (An alphabetic or "acrostic" poem is one whose sentences begin with successive letters of the alphabet.)

Much, much more would have to be said on this subject of misogyny in the Bible, and particularly in these books of proverbs, to cover the subject adequately. It merits book-length discussion, which it has, indeed, received. For our purposes here, we make one final comment: If the faults of women are bluntly exposed, so are the faults of men. The men are at even greater length indicated to be at times liars; thieves; double-dealing, treacherous friends; cheating business partners; drunken carousers; lazy, unreliable gossip-mongers, and worse. Hence, the candid admission of biblical displeasure at *some women's* conduct should receive the addendum that the identical displeasure is indicated for *some men's* conduct, and at greater length. Is the balance of praise and condemnation equal? Judge for yourself!

2. *CHILDREN.* The advice for rearing children is quite unequivocal. Strict discipline is inculcated, at the risk of raising a spoiled, ungrateful upstart. The emphasis on physical punishment would receive raised eyebrows in our day, particularly in phrases such as, "Beat him!" referring to the son in the family.

3. *MONEY.* The policy of biblical proverbs concerning the use of money is first, last, and always, conservative. Interestingly enough, you will find contrary advice. In some proverbs, the generosity in going bond for a neighbor is praised. In others, strong warnings are expressed against giving a loan to anyone.

4. *ALCOHOLIC DRINK.* It is rather well known that one cannot find an unequivocal condemnation of alcoholic drink as such anywhere in the Bible. Here in the proverbs the condemnation extends to drunkenness and carousing. The description of red wine in the goblet going down the throat smoothly, yet leading to boasts to fight the world as on the deck of a ship at sea, is as applicable to our own day as it was then—including the blunt description of the feelings on the "morning after."

5. *FRIENDS.* False friends and true friends alike come in for their share of notice; again, the analysis of human nature is timeless.

6. *SLAVERY.* Although there is not too much space devoted to this topic, the incidental proverbs referring to runaway slaves and proper treat-

ment for slaves remind us that slavery was taken for granted as a cultural fact.

7. *COMMERCE.* The attitude for the marketplace is amply indicated by the warnings against false weights and—"it is difficult for a merchant to avoid committing evil, and for a tradesman not to incur sin"!

8. *DINNER ETIQUETTE.* Of all the earthy advice, the biblical proverbs seem to excel in their candor on this point.

9. *GOSSIP.* Earlier we mentioned how much attention has been given to the biblical proverbs for their apparent emphasis on faults in women. However, their repeated and lengthy tirades against faults of the tongue are directed far more against men than against women. "A curse on the scandal-monger!"

10. *RICHES AND POVERTY.* The contempt of the rich for the poor seems almost to be taken for granted in these proverbs. The biblical texts repeatedly urge almsgiving and mercy to the needy.

The Song of Songs (Song of Solomon)

READ: this short book in its entirety.

The insertion of the Song of Songs into the biblical canon of inspired works has in all centuries been a reason for questioning. The work is certainly a collection of wedding songs, with strong sensuous and erotic references, and with no mention of God. How and why was it included in the canon?

Probably the most basic reason was the book's praise for holy married love, blessed by God, and therefore good. Difficulties against this thinking were raised by ancient rabbis and later by early Fathers of the Church, who preferred to see in it an allegory of God's love for His people Israel, or the love of Christ for His church. In our day the interpretation has prevailed that these were placed here precisely as songs of married love. Another reason suggested is the frequent negative references to woman in other wisdom literature. The picture of woman here is so laudatory that it certainly serves to balance that other picture of the shameless adulteress and the selfish nag.

It has been conjectured that a mistranslation of Song of Songs 8, 5 led to the misunderstanding that an apple was the forbidden fruit in the garden of Eden. The verse actually says, "Under the apple tree your mother conceived you." An earlier translation was circulated thus, "Under the apple tree was your mother corrupted."

The Book of Jonah

Speaking generally, all the biblical titles listed among the prophets are writings BY prophets. That is why it is rather a curious anomaly that Jonah is found with the other eleven "Minor Prophets," even though Jonah is a short book ABOUT a prophet.

READ: all four chapters of the Book of Jonah.

Even fifteen hundred years ago, some of the Fathers of the Church saw reasons to consider Jonah a type of parable rather than an account of strict history. This opinion, more or less prevailing in our day, is based not on the supposed difficulty for Jonah to be swallowed by a "whale," but rather on the repeated qualities that point to a parabolic rather than a literally actual interpretation.

The four chapters stand practically by themselves. When the action in one is completed, the characters and milieu disappear, and only Jonah continues on into the other. The book is certainly of Jewish origin, and certainly from the time after the Exile. Its most prominent characteristic is its emphasis on the generosity of God's mercy that extends to all peoples, not merely to the chosen Jews. For that reason, scholars have looked on Jonah as a Jewish polemic against Jewish exaggerated nationalism and exclusive theology.

The chapters can easily be summarized thus:

1) Jonah on the sea;
2) Jonah in the fish;
3) Jonah in Nineveh;
4) Jonah angry and petulant.

The biting satire begins immediately. Jonah, a "good" prophet, does not wish to carry the message of conversion to pagans so evil as those at Nineveh, the capital of Assyria. He has decided it is useless. God tells Jonah to go east to Nineveh; Jonah goes west, deliberately, to Tarshish, the limits of the then known world (apparently modern Cadiz, Spain). During the storm, the pagan sailors call on their pagan gods while the Hebrew prophet lies fast asleep. The pagan sailors are so responsible as to be reluctant to throw Jonah into the sea. When the sea resumes its calm, it is the pagan sailors who offer sacrifices to the one true God.

The great fish appears as a literary vehicle or symbol of the encompassing providence of God. Within the belly of the fish, Jonah offers a prayer of thanksgiving for his safety (someone has called this prayer somewhat premature!). After the fish has vomited Jonah on dry land, the call of the Lord comes again. This time, when Jonah does preach in Nineveh, the prophet becomes greatly discomfited because his message of penance is heard and heeded. Finally, the Lord treats Jonah like a sulking child when He compares Jonah's anger at having lost a trivial shady vine with the genuine catastrophe that would have occurred had these myriads of people perished. The book ends with a striking rhetorical question placed in the mouth of God, "Shall I not have pity?"

The lesson, of course, is clear: We should not prefer *our* way of achieving religious goals to the ultimate goal of God's glory according to God's will. A final reason for considering Jonah a parable is that nowhere in history does there appear the slightest turning of Assyria to the God of the Hebrews, certainly not four hundred years before Jonah was written.

THE CLOSING OF THE OLD TESTAMENT (Maccabees)

From the time of Ezra and Nehemiah (c. 433 B.C.), the Jews had maintained their existence as a Persian province. Renewed emphasis was given to the Law and to the ritual of the Temple, now that the nation no longer figured as even a minor political power on the stage of history. An apparently peaceful and uneventful stretch of more than 200 years followed.

This peace was broken by a chain of outside events. Persia fell before a new force from the West. Alexander the Great added Palestine and Syria to the expanding Greek empire in 331 B.C. At his death a few years later, the empire was divided among four of his generals. At first Palestine fell to the Ptolemies who ruled the Egyptian section of Alexander's former empire and were inclined to be tolerant of the Hebrew religion and way of life.

In 198 B.C. Palestine was annexed to the Syrian segment of Alexander's empire ruled by the Seleucids, descendants of Seleucus, one of the four generals. Their policy was one of enforced cultural and religious conformity. Everyone must become Greek in language, culture, and religion. A steady pressure was exerted on the reluctant elements among the Jews to become Greek in this way. (This process is called "Hellenizing," after the ancient name of Greece, "Hellas.") The pressure exploded in 168 B.C. when Antiochus Epiphanes IV desecrated the temple at Jerusalem by introducing the worship of Zeus, the "father-god" of the many Greek gods and goddesses, into the holy precincts.

The sacrilegious act was not taken lying down. A leading Jewish family, the Hasmoneans, better known to us by the nickname "Maccabees" (it probably means "hammer") launched a revolt which was to rage for thirty years. For the first time since the days of the divided Jewish kingdom some 500 years before, the Jews tasted the meaning of military success and political importance.

READ: The first book of Maccabees, 1-4, 6, 8, 14.

Here we find an extremely vigorous account of the attempts of the Maccabees (Mattathias and his five sons) to maintain the Jewish religion and way of life by force of arms. The account was written a little more than a hundred years before the birth of Christ by a supporter of the Hasmoneans. The author was a resident of Jerusalem, and even by Western standards was an excellent historian. He seems to have been an eyewitness of many of the events he narrates. His book covers the forty years from the beginning of the revolt to the death of the last of the Maccabean brothers, Simon.

The Book of Maccabees is an important link between Old and New Testament times. Together with the other late books of the Old Testament, it forms a prelude and background to the gospels. In it we already find evident three outstanding characteristics of Judaism that appeared in the time of Christ as well:

a) a profound consciousness of God's supremacy over His creation;
b) an unbreakable attachment to the Temple and the Holy City;
c) complete fidelity to the observance of the Law.

Yet the pious Jew had to learn that political eminence was not the way in which the "blessings for all nations" promised by God to come through Abraham's descendants could be realized. The eminence faded away almost as quickly as it had arrived. In 63 B.C., the Roman general Pompey conquered Jerusalem.

Highpoints of these selections:

"THE HELLENIZERS" (1 Mc 1, 11-16)

Not all the Jews were adamantly opposed to the Greek Way. Not a few felt that the wiser course was to cooperate and curry favor, while a great many more had a real admiration for Greek ways and wanted to combine them with Hebraic culture to the improvement of both. The risk to Jewish identity, however, was tremendous. Some Jewish men went so far (as Maccabees relates) to undergo a savage bit of primitive surgery to attempt to erase the evidence of their physical circumcision.

THE PIOUS ONES (1 Mc 2, 42)

The "Hassidim" or Pious Ones were the forerunners of the Pharisees of the gospels, arising at this time to join the Maccabees in their revolt.

THE FEAST OF DEDICATION (1 Mc 4, 36-59)

The event described was commemorated for future generations by the feast of Hannukah, or "lights." This feast is still celebrated by modern Jews and falls in late December. It is mentioned in the New Testament in Jn 10, 22.

THE ALLIANCE WITH ROME (1 Mc 8, 1-32)

Most of us have heard the old saying of Arabs, "Never let the camel get his nose under the tent, for if he does, he will be sleeping inside and you will be out in the cold." This observation was borne out in the case of the Roman alliance with the Jews. The treaty was the first step which inevitably led to the fall of Jerusalem to Pompey in 63 B.C. Rome had never had any intention of supplying the promised military aid. The treaty was merely an attempt to embarrass the Seleucid monarchs by recognizing their rebellious province as a nation.

The Book of Daniel

When the first excitement of the Maccabean revolt had spent itself, some time around 163 B.C., many of the people had second thoughts. So far the revolt had been astoundingly successful, but what did the future hold in store? They had bested a small Syrian army, little more than military police, but how would they fare against the full power of the mighty Seleucid Empire?

It seems to have been at a time such as this that a now unknown Jew gathered various traditions about a certain Hebrew named Daniel, who had lived through similar difficulties during the days of the exile four hundred years earlier, so the traditions said.

READ: The Book of Daniel, 1-7, 13-14.

In our Bibles the Book of Daniel is included among the Major Prophets. Strictly speaking, the book does not belong to the prophetical school of writing. Moreover, it had the peculiar quality of often being "prophecy after the event." In other words, Daniel again and again speaks of past political and military situations, yet relates them as if they had been prophesied beforehand.

The accusation has been made at times that this would be falsehood; but if the literary form were known to be "prophecy after the event" as such, then it would be no more false to its hearers and readers than a historical novel, known to be fiction within a historical framework.

The Book of Daniel thus might be called in modern parlance a pamphlet "of the resistance movement." Its purpose was to encourage the faithful Jew, and it contained clues to this effect which its countrymen would understand.

Edifying Events and Visions

The Book of Daniel falls into two main parts. Chapters 1 to 6, and 13 and 14 contain various traditional accounts familiar to the first readers. The author has carefully selected the events with an eye to their appropriateness to the trying circumstances of his countrymen. In all these events the God of Daniel always triumphs.

The second half of the book (chapters 7 through 12) employs a quite different literary form. Here the author conveys to his readers under the form of various visions his theology of history for which he had already prepared them. The various symbolic images employed were largely familiar ones, frequently found in the prophets, especially in Ezechiel. We are shown a struggle between the forces of good and evil. Then, God intervenes in a decisive triumph which brings everything to a climactic resolution. This in turn inaugurates the Divine Kingdom by a general judgment and resurrection.

This type of literary form is called "apocalyptic," and is very puzzling to us moderns. You will find it recurring in the New Testament in the Apocalypse, the Book of Revelations. Its most disconcerting feature is its constant use of metaphorical language to an extent that is most unusual in ordinary speech. Symbols are the regular thing, symbolic numbers add up to symbolic conclusions, and standard stylized phraseology recurs throughout.

The alleged author presents visions which he himself cannot understand until angels or mysterious voices come on the scene to interpret the visions. The message is projected into the future, from an apparent turning point in the past; and usually all this is presented under the name of some great personage other than the anonymous author.

The important thing for us moderns to remember in reading apocalyptic is that this is not our customary way of speaking or thinking. We must take pains to find the code or cipher, so that we can see all this in the light in which it was written, and when written, then understood by its contemporaries.

For example, very often apocalyptic will speak of a "horn" of a beast when it means the power of an enemy, anti-religious kingdom. The reason for this symbol was the fact that the strength and power of animals lay in the ability of their horns to act as offense and defense. Time lapses are discussed in terms of round numbers, symbolically. Fire in particular will refer to the power of God, not necessarily in a destroying or punishing sense, but sometimes as purifying.

HIGHPOINTS OF THESE SELECTIONS (Dn 1, 1 ff.)

Each of the first six chapters of Daniel is a complete event in itself. All are drawn from the period of the Babylonian exile (587-538 B.C.). However, not all details are in complete accord with the history of the time, even though they are presented as if they had been written exactly in those times. The lesson of the chapters lies in one fact: God is faithful, and Jews often highly placed in pagan courts followed the presciptions of the Law in most difficult circumstances.

THE DIETARY LAWS (Dn 1, 8)

Here the author makes allusion to the practice among Jews of regarding only certain foods as proper for a Son of the Covenant. Such foods are referred to as "clean" or ritually pure, as "kosher." That Daniel chose what might seem to us a rather secondary point of law upon which to take issue with his pagan masters, might seem strange. However, to an orthodox Jew these dietary laws were an external concrete sign of loyalty to God.

THE IMAGE OF GOLD (Dn 3, 1 ff.)

Notice the quaint, utterly unique style of this chapter. Practically nowhere else in the Bible can one find such a constant repetition of the same phrases when pronouns and summations would have done the job just as well. This chapter has been pointed out as an example of the master story teller before an audience which delights in every detail of the story, so much so as to ask that it be strung out.

DANIEL'S VISION (Dn 7)

Here, in verse 13 is the striking reference to the "son of man," a term Jesus will use many years later as a means of describing Himself as the promised savior, without, however, using the politically compromising term of Messiah itself.

DANIEL THE JUDGE (Ch. 13, 14)

It seems probable that these two chapters were added at a later date by some unknown author to the Daniel collection. Their theme is still the same: Great is the God of Daniel! For your interest in making a classification of all the literary forms contained in the Bible, you can now read these chapters as the primitive ancestors of the modern detective story: how to break down the story of lying witnesses, and how to prove fraud and collusion by the use of circumstantial evidence—ash-dust, used to trap the evidence of the footsteps of the deceivers!

Unit 3. The New Testament

In the general Introduction we mentioned that a number of significantly new approaches had been introduced by scholars into the area of biblical studies. One of these is the consideration that the New Testament should not be looked on *merely* as the fulfillment of the Old, nor the Old looked on *merely* as a preparation for the New. The New Testament should not be divorced from the Old; instead, the two Testaments should be read as a continuity, since the outlook of the New is completely built on the foundation of the Old.

Other differences do, however, exist. The Old Testament spanned almost twenty centuries in its traditions and ten centuries in its writing. The New spans less than a century in its tradition as well as in its writing.

Twenty-seven separate compositions make up the New Testament, rather inaccurately designated as "books." Their order, as they appear in modern Bibles has no direct relationship with the order of their composition. In this respect, a casual reader is somewhat misled into getting the impression that the four Gospels came first, then the Acts of the Apostles, then the Pauline and other epistles, and last of all, the Book of Revelation or Apocalypse.

No arrangement is completely satisfactory if you would wish to sample all the New Testament writings in their proper order. For one thing, we are not completely certain of accurate dates of origin. Also, materials of different age have certainly been brought together in the same work. Finally, unanimous agreement of scholarship rarely exists on all these points.

Understanding the conditions of probability and conjecture, we can suggest the following detailed chronology of the New Testament, adding to what was already given in the general Introduction:

6 B.C.—Birth of Jesus Christ, spring;
4 B.C.—Death of Herod the Great;
27 A.D.—Beginning of public ministry of Jesus;
30 A.D.—Death and resurrection of Jesus;
After 36 A.D.: Conversion of Paul;
50 A.D. ff.: Written sources of Jesus' words and works in existence;
First drafts of Mark's Gospel;
Earliest traditions in writing, later found in John's Gospel;
1 & 2 Thessalonians;

55 A.D. ff.: Galatians;
1 & 2 Corinthians;
Romans;
Philippians;
60 A.D. ff.: Colossians;
Ephesians;
Gospel of Mark;
70 A.D. ff.: Gospel of Matthew;
Gospel of Luke;
Acts of Apostles;
Hebrews;
90 A.D. ff.: Final form of Gospel of John;
Apocalypse;
100 to 125 A.D. at the latest: 2 Peter, last book of the New Testament.

The Gospels

Before you begin to read the Gospels, it is extremely important that you are aware of the kind of literature they are. Nowhere else in the bible is it more necessary to apply the principle of understanding literary forms properly.

The four gospels should be identified as just that: "gospels." No other literature in history, whether sacred or secular, parallels them. They do discuss historical fact, and they are historical; but they look at history in their own special way. They are certainly not tape-recordings of the words of Jesus, or word-films of the actions of Jesus. They are definitely interpretations of what they tell. They are not so much arguments for their readers to have faith; instead, they are intended to strengthen the faith which they presume is at least rudimentary in their audience. Again and again, they will look at a historical event in the life of Jesus in the light of faith in His completed mission which at the time of the event had not yet occurred.

Why is this awareness of the nature of the four gospels so critically important? One reason is to protect the modern student like yourself from making mistakes at either end of the spectrum. On the one hand, you might believe that Christian faith obliges you to accept each and every word of the gospel slavishly as "gospel truth," so that any interpretation or shading of its meaning would appear to be a denial of religious truth. Hence, it might be a source of grave shock to you and to others to read in the public press or in full-length gospel commentaries opinions of scholars that appear to deny the existence of miracles, angels, or even the divinity of Jesus. In many cases these scripture scholars are thoroughly orthodox in their religious faith. All they are saying in some of these cases which "hit the headlines" is that certain texts of the gospels do not of themselves prove or indicate a point of faith contained in the Christian creed. This does not necessarily constitute a denial of the creed, which often incorporates a tradition over and above the mere wording of a gospel text.

But you can easily make the mistake in the other direction as well, of becoming overly sceptical of the apparent context of the gospels. "A little knowledge is a dangerous thing." The professional Christian scripture scholar can be aware of the sharp distinction between creed in Christian belief and strict interpretation of an individual gospel text. A less trained reader might miss this distinction, and end up bereft of all faith in the gospels, and this would be the greater tragedy.

Like all books of the bible, the four gospels originated from a period of earlier oral traditions coupled with progressive editing and progressive merging with further traditions. We possess only the end product, yet it is not difficult even for the amateur eye to note occasional stage directions that must have been inserted for a later audience at a later time. As an example, you can be certain that the original Jewish audiences which heard the words of Jesus did not need the regular asides which succeeding tradition added, so that the later non-Jewish audience could understand the contemporary Jewish customs at the time of Jesus. (e.g. Mark 7, 3-4, 11, 19)

As a minor exercise in attentiveness, you might find the gospels even more interesting for yourself by developing the habit of noting these explanatory asides that came from later days than the original events.

The Synoptic Problem

The three gospels of Matthew, Mark, and Luke incorporate a centuries-old and celebrated difficulty for interpretation which is called the "Synoptic Problem." The word "synoptic" comes from the fact that these three gospels parallel each other so well that they can often be scanned at a glance in three columns to discern their closeness—from the Greek, *syn—opsis* "with a glance". The term has no connotation whatsoever of a synopsis in the sense of capsule comments.

But the close parallels are at the same time loaded with repeated discrepancies in emphasis, details, and apparent chronology or lack of it. This situation exists, of course, only for Matthew, Mark, and Luke, since John's gospel has always been recognized in a class by itself.

It is no solution of the difficulty to look for the so-called "easy way out," and say that one of the three gospels has the correct nuance, and that the others are somehow wrong. A typical example can be found in the story of the cure of a blind man, Bartimaeus, outside Jericho. Mark (10, 46) gives the name of the blind beggar and says that the cure happened when Jesus was leaving Jericho. Matthew (20, 29) says that Jesus cured two blind men (no names) as he was leaving Jericho. Luke (18, 35) says that Jesus cured one blind man (no name) as Jesus approached Jericho. Nor can we suppose that these were actually three separate events, in view of the other circumstances and words that are practically identical in all three accounts.

Many answers have been given to this question of the Synoptic Problem, of which we select the main answers here. The first point to note is that oral tradition may well have emphasized only the main points of its story. Side details were considered insignificant, and the final written gospel version carried with it this lack of interest in the details.

Other answers are drawn from the dependence of the finished gospels on earlier written documents. Some of this dependence is only tentative and probable, since it demands the existence of previous writings not in our possession or in our knowledge. Other dependence is quite certain, as, for example, the fact that Luke must have used Mark as one of his sources. The problems occur when we consider the added independent material which each evangelist brought to his gospel, plus the question why at one point or other each evangelist will go his own way in emphasizing, interpreting, or selecting his material.

We will not enter here into the intricacies of all the theories that have been proposed—two-source theory, three-source theory, single document for threefold tradition, complementary document for twofold tradition, or multiple documentation for the whole complex.

The very fact that so many theories have been brought forward with no one theory winning general acceptance seems to be adequate proof that no one knows the final answer. The consensus seems to be that all theories are partially true. Probably the final answer may be the fact that something of the interdependence mentioned in each of the theories occurred to some extent or other.

What should be stated as quite solid is that there must have existed some written collections of Jesus' words (and actions?) before the gospels. This hypothetical collection or set of collections has been sometimes called "Q"—from the German word for source, *quelle.*

Another solid conclusion is that a primitive gospel under the influence of Matthew existed in the Aramaic language, and that it has long been lost. Next came the gospel of Mark in the Greek, generally accepted as the earliest of all. After that, Luke, and finally, the present Greek gospel of Matthew. This Greek Matthew was far more than a mere translation of the original Aramaic Matthew; it is an interpretation as well, plus a mass of new material gained from other sources.

Where does the gospel of St. John fit into this scheme? No serious scholarship denies that the finished gospel of John is the last, and that it appeared toward the end of the first century. The point which is receiving more and more attention, however, is the fact that John is a mosaic document, perhaps even more than Mark, Luke, and Matthew. It definitely bears the imprint of the man who was John the Apostle, but it also bears imprints of later hands referring to John as the "disciple whom Jesus loved," and successive layers of explanatory comments for people in places far removed from the original scenes in Judea and Galilee. Earlier scholars used to think that John, written as the latest gospel, acted only as an "end product." More and more modern interpretation sees in John strands of tradition which appear to be as primitive and early as any that we possess in Mark or even in early St. Paul.

As you read the four gospels (in as much detail as you have time for), keep your eye open to note the distinctive styles and emphasis. The Synoptics place most of the ministry of Jesus in Galilee, with little attempt at chronology. John emphasizes the ministry in Jerusalem, the city. The Synoptics portray a Jesus of many actions and fewer words. The Jesus in John speaks in a different, profound style. Many miracle stories appear in the Synoptics, rather briefly put; John relates only a few miracles but at great length.

In the Synoptics, the adversaries of Jesus are usually the Sadducees and Pharisees, listed as a group. In John, the adversaries appear occasionally as "the Jews."

We should linger on this point for a moment, since misunderstanding of the literary usages concerning Pharisees and "the Jews" has caused much anti-Semitic feeling in history, and without cause. The quarrels of Jesus with the Pharisees can logically be interpreted as typical rabbinical discussions of their day, on points of doctrine or morals. The references to "the Jews" in John need even more qualification, because the phrase, "the Jews" appears in four or five different connotations.

Certainly, as far as referring to those who hate Jesus and his work, "the Jews" then applies to the leaders of the people, and that at Jerusalem. In other places, "the Jews" is a neutral reference to Jewish customs for non-Jewish readers. Elsewhere (as at the death and revivification of Lazarus at Bethany) the phrase refers even to friends of Mary, Martha, Lazarus, and evidently, friends of Jesus. Finally, as in the discussion with the Samaritan woman at the well, "the Jews" is a designation of the peoples living in the southernmost province of the Holy Land, in distinction to the Samaritans, their historical enemies and dissident "Protestants."

Our conclusion must be that all Pharisees and all "the Jews" should not be branded as hostile to Jesus. It was from both these groups that Jesus drew his followers. Enlightened ecumenical leadership has called on all of us to see ourselves with our own typical human faults appearing in the faults of the enemies of Jesus, not to point the accusing finger only at others and never at ourselves.

The Infancy Narratives

READ: Matthew 1, 2; Luke 1, 2.

Probably in no other area of the gospels is the suggestion more pertinent which we mentioned in the preceding pages: that you, as a student of the New Testament, would not veer to either extreme in the interpretation of the Infancy Narratives, because of reading apparently iconoclastic interpretations (popularly called "debunking") that appear in the public press.

These first two chapters of Matthew and Luke are receiving more attention than ever before. They are not only very different in character from the rest of the gospels, but, we should note, are very different among themselves. They would appear to have been joined to the stories of Jesus' public ministry, passion, death, and resurrection last of all. The ultimate answer to the problems of interpretation which they present may well lie in that fact. In other words, they speak of the early life of Jesus in terms of his full manifestation and glorification after his resurrection. Instead of the obscurity which undoubtedly existed during his childhood, they speak of Jesus as already known to many and received by many as the saving Lord.

It is this ambivalent atmosphere toward obscurity which has led so many scholars to say that the Infancy Narratives have "theologized" early stories of Jesus so as to present his gospel teaching, as it were, from the very beginning. Yet the one foundational fact of history is that Jesus began in obscurity, preached in relative obscurity, and died the same way—a common malefactor, who ran afoul of the authorities.

To oversimplify the various approaches to the Infancy Narratives, we might suggest that some of the approaches read only symbolism into these stories with no historical background, and others read only history into these stories with no symbolism. The position we present here grants the existence of symbolical and hyperbolical language—language sometimes exaggerated in order to make a point strongly. But we insist just as strongly that the historical basis of the Infancy Narratives is so strongly intertwined in the narratives of Matthew and Luke that it would be foolish to dismiss it with a blithe wave of the hand as merely fanciful imagination. There will inevitably be some disagreement on precisely where the historical begins and ends, and where the moralizing or theologizing or teaching of lessons begins and ends; but the historical has to be there in order to explain the constant agreements in Matthew and Luke both with each other and with secular customs and history.

One of the difficulties you will hear is the question concerning the origin of these traditions of Jesus' childhood. No scholars deny that Matthew emphasizes the position of Joseph and Luke emphasizes the position of Mary. Unfortunately, because there are few if any other sources of these traditions available, the tendency has arisen to throw doubt on the historicity of the Infancy Narratives. Such an argument, however, is unfair. It forgets that the traditions on the spot first had the right to credence. It is our ignorance of those traditions that is at fault, not the traditions themselves. We have no right to distrust the traditions merely because we do not know how they came to us with this knowledge about Mary and Joseph.

READ: Matthew 1, 1-17:

Matthew begins his first chapter with a genealogy of Jesus that is a perfect imitation of the Old Testament genealogy. What we said about the genealogies in Genesis holds true here for Matthew as well: that the biblical genealogy is not intended primarily as a list of physical births, but that it has a teaching or didactic value as well. It is not necessarily intended to be complete; it can include additional characters as well, in order to teach its lesson—as Matthew does with his three groups of fourteen generations apiece.

The Matthean genealogy has always been conspicuous for its abrupt change in phraseology as the birth of Jesus was to be described: "Matthan begot Jacob, Jacob begot Joseph, the husband of Mary, of whom Jesus was born, who is called Chirst."

READ: Matthew 1, 18-23:

One tremendously important historical aspect of the Infancy Narratives calls for explicit mention here. Both Matthew and Luke can be well understood when we place their two accounts in the perspective of Mary's espousal to Joseph. We have to rid ourselves of any occidental modern idea that this was some sort of engagement; it was not. Instead, the marriage customs of the time dictated a two or three-part ceremony. The future husband would pay the dowry price to the father of the bride; then would begin the year of espousal, during which time the couple would not live together, yet they would be legally considered husband and wife. The girl was bound to loyalty to her espoused husband under pain of being called an adulteress. If the man died, the girl would be considered a widow.

At the end of the espousal, the third ceremony would take place: the "wedding," when the groom would publicly go with his friends to the home of the bride, where she was waiting with her girl attendants, and then escort her into his own home.

As far as we can ascertain, pregnancy and conception during the year of espousal was usually not to occur; but other evidence indicates that if the bride became pregnant during these months, the child was considered legitimate if the espoused husband accepted the baby as his own.

Joseph's predicament thus comes into focus. God interferes in the private life of Mary, the espoused wife of Joseph, and gives her the Messiah son. Mary's reaction is unknown to us. Out of justice to her espoused husband, she would seem to be forced to say something, lest he enter a marriage where a child appeared he would know not to be his own by generation. On the other hand, it is very possible that Mary was not aware that her secret was to be shared even with her beloved husband. She had her own Gethsemani; as a single girl now espoused, how could she explain something so beyond human experience? Did God wish this?

Joseph's Gethsemani has been acknowledged from earliest Christian centuries, despite the obscurity which otherwise surrounded Joseph. No one could read the Matthean narrative without noting Joseph's hesitancy in taking action. He did not know which way to turn. On the one hand, to keep an unfaithful wife was to condone adultery; on the other, to dismiss Mary, whom he could not believe to have been unfaithful, seemed equally unjust. This interpretation of Joseph's doubt seems most likely, although the two other extremes have appeared in history: namely, either that Joseph actually did suspect adultery, or that he guessed Mary's miraculous pregnancy and out of (false?) humility wished to be out of the picture by divorcing her!

From the time of the Fathers of the Church centuries ago, Matthew's words have been noted on this special point: "Mary was found, before they came together, to be with child by the Holy Spirit." No one has satisfactorily explained how this did occur. It might be an answer that Mary somehow let Joseph know of her pregnancy, perhaps without being able to tell him the cause. Matthew does not give any detailed account as to how Mary was with child; Luke will give the scene rich commentary.

The one element emerging from the Matthean account is that the virginal conception of Jesus in Mary occurred in obscurity, known only to Mary. Eventually, Joseph also was informed through some fashion of God's plan.

READ: Matthew, 2

No portion of the Infancy Narrative has been more derided for its alleged lack of historical content than the account of the Magi. Yet, even here we should pause to note the innumerable historical links which are involved. Certainly, we cannot and should not deny the many examples of strong writing that argue against the obscurity of the events: "All Jerusalem was troubled," and "King Herod assembled all the chief priests and scribes." But these details cannot of themselves destroy the continuing historical fabric.

This is not the place to repeat a lengthy and detailed defense of the "natural-star" theory, but we mention it here as a counterpoise to the adverse publicity that speaks of the star of the Magi as something merely symbolic and conceived out of the fertile imagination of an early Matthean writer.

Briefly put, the natural-star theory suggests that the Magi were, as their name indicates, Zoroastrian priest-astrologers from Arabia or from Persia. Their beliefs would lead them to search the heavens for planetary (not astral or "star") signs. When the planets were in "conjunction," passing each other, a time of special influence was believed to be happening. Thus, the historical fact exists that Saturn and Jupiter passed each other three times in reverse fashion two or three months apart, during 7 B.C., and this very unusual progression and regression occurred in the constellation called "Pisces," allocated as the "House of the Hebrews" to reflect the fortunes of the tiny Jewish people. Next, in early 6 B.C., Mars joined the rather unusual grouping of Saturn and Jupiter in the early morning sky.

The reasoning behind this theory is that the astrologers saw something that made sense only to them: an unusual sign in the heavens, suggesting that something unusual had happened among the Jews—but, we repeat, unusual to them alone as astrologers watching planetary motions. On that basis, they would travel to Jerusalem the capital of the Jews, to find if the rumored Messiah had been born. They would *not* follow their star; they already had decided that Jerusalem was their goal from another reason as its position as the Jewish capital.

This has been the nucleus of the theory of the "natural star." On this basis, several non-Jews of good will would have followed the light of their conscience to look for a newborn Messiah. How the tradition would have grown, and how the tradition would have reached the author of the Matthean chapter we have no way of knowing; but the possibility should be objectively explored before the entire second chapter is discarded as mere symbolism, empty of all historic reality.

For that matter, a dismissal of the Magi story would also entail wholesale dismissal of the flight into Egypt and the massacre of the baby boys at Bethlehem—two items that bear all the earmarks of a genuine event. It has been an unworthy argument to claim that the massacre of the Bethlehm babies could not have occurred because we have no other historical testimony to that effect. In an era when all life was cheap, when a tyrant like Herod could destroy as he pleased, so insignificant an affair as the butchery of thirty boys in a tiny hamlet would hardly merit recording in the palace archives.

READ: Luke 1, 1-4.

We now turn to the other source of the Infancy Narratives: the gospel of Luke. Its first four verses ought to give pause to anyone rashly imputing its credibility. Luke very explicitly lays down the rules he followed to gather his evidence, to evaluate it, and "to write an orderly account" of it. The burden of proof should always be on those who deny the Lucan historicity, for their necessity to indicate why they reject so much. We always must return to the fact that Luke uses a literary form of historical basis, with an interpretation of biblical theologizing that is being more and more recognized as deliberate and anything but falsifying.

READ: Luke 1, 5-25.

For us, an interesting point to note is that Luke's account of the conception and birth of John the Baptist will have noticeable parallels in Luke's succeeding account of the conception and birth of Jesus.

READ: Luke 1, 26-80.

From a literary viewpoint, the Lucan narrative of the annunciation to Mary and Mary's visitation to Elizabeth is pure genius, for its vivid detail, its succinct development of action, and for its constant hearkening to Old Testament parallels in order to find words for these actions.

The mention of the angel Gabriel in the annunciation has been decried, as unhistorical, by some. An answer to this might be: How can any human hold God to one or other method of action? If God wishes to make His will known to any of His creatures, who is to say nay? The rather distressing ridicule of the Annunciation narrative, as if an "angel in white bed clothes with flipflopping wings" appeared to Mary completely misses the point, distorts the narrative, and is unjust to the Lucan gospel. The angel bringing God's message to Mary is just that: an angel, a messenger. Beyond that fact, we are not misled into any fanciful description of how God would send such a message to Mary.

When you read the "Magnificat" anthem of Mary in verses 47-55, you should note that this is just one more instance of the various canticles Luke has inserted into his gospel. Others occur in the mouth of Zechariah, and Simeon in the temple as well. Later, we will encounter Luke's regular usage in the Acts of the Apostles, whereby speeches are put into the mouths of persons, not so much on the basis that these people had to utter these very words, but that the situation was such which would well be described in such words. Such a custom among ancient authors was common, and is well authenticated. It does not connote mendacity; it rather emphasizes the thoughts that must have been present at such a time, to describe the occasion and the reaction properly.

READ: Luke 2.

The Christmas story is so well known that one would imagine it could well go without further comment. The deplorable aspect is that it has been overlain with centuries of romantic legend which has little or no basis in the Lucan narrative.

For one thing, the ninety-mile journey from Nazareth in the north to Bethlehem in the south could hardly have been a hasty, last-minute decision on the part of Joseph and Mary. Mary was practically at term. Luke also says that her days were accomplished "*while* they were still there" at Bethlehem. The reference to swaddling-clothes as the layette of the baby indicates Mary was ready and waiting for Jesus to be born. Luke certainly gives short shrift to the medieval legend of the hard-hearted innkeeper, turning away a poverty-stricken couple. The "inn" of Bethlehem would hardly be more than a stockade barricaded for safety against robbers at night. Since there was no room "for them," the implication may well be one of delicacy: the inn was not a suitable place for Jesus to be born. The reference to the manger implies a living place where animals (such as a cow or donkey) may also have been present.

Again, the presence of the angels in Luke's nativity account has drawn expressions of disbelief from various commentators. We can only state again that the birth of Jesus is certainly drawn in lines that would point to far more prominence than would be expected for this child. None the less, Luke is describing the prominence of the birth of Jesus as fully deserved, for all that Jesus already meant by his coming into the world.

READ: Luke 3, 23-38:

We close this section of commentary on Luke's opening chapters with this genealogy of Jesus. It is an excellent example of our need to understand the literary forms intended by the gospel writers. On the surface, Luke's genealogy of Jesus would appear to be in flat contradiction to Matthew's genealogy, which has a different line of intermediate ancestors. Various hypotheses have been suggested to explain the difference, but from repeated experience with learning the deeper meaning of literary forms in the gospels, it would be a fatal mistake to claim that either Luke or Matthew had to be in complete error in their traditions as to the origin of Jesus. It is our ignorance that does not know how to reconcile the accounts.

The Parables

READ: as much of the gospels from the Infancy Narratives to the Passion as suits your time and interest. Most of this material is self-explanatory, and easily grasped. However, we are selecting references to the parables of Jesus for special comment, in view of the nuances involved in this kind of literary form.

On their surface many of the parables present a deceptive appearance of simplicity, as if the mind of a child could plumb them to their depths at once. It is only upon further and more careful reading that one notices surface obscurities, contrasts, paradoxes, unexpected conclusions.

One possible source of confusion can be removed at once by defining the parable at its root. There are parables in the strict sense of the word and parables in a wide sense, condensed into proverbial phrases or sayings. The strict meaning of the English word "parable" does not adequately convey the use of the parable as Jesus exemplified it to perfection.

We sometimes distinguish between a parable and an allegory on the basis that the parable contains the general idea of a comparison, while the allegory constitutes an extended metaphor, whereby every detail tells some truth by its comparison.

The Hebrew parable on the other hand went much farther, indicating a short saying of profound meaning. We come closer to its meaning by considering it as a "literary device used to illustrate a moral or religious truth by means of an imaginary but entirely plausible fact."

Some principles should be kept in mind throughout:

1) There is usually a principal lesson developed by the comparison, but secondary details should be recognized as such and should not be given precedence over the principal lesson.

2) Very often, literary details are inserted which have the purpose of making the story sound more natural and easy flowing, but in themselves they could be dropped without harming the imagery or the lesson.

3) In general the parables of Jesus will describe the course of nature, but they are not obliged to follow such reality down to the last detail. An example of this type which has drawn interested comment is the gospel sentence that a good tree does not bear bad fruit and a bad tree does not bear good fruit. Strictly speaking, this is not so; none the less, a poor tree does not produce as much good fruit as does a healthy tree.

4) Some parables end with an apparent conclusion which should not be interpreted as part of their main lesson. There can appear a maxim or a proverb such as "Many are called but few are chosen" or "The first shall be last" (cf. Matthew 22, 14; 20, 16). We have to note each instance individually, since these apparent conclusions are often additions which the early gospel tradition had to place somewhere, and sometimes was no longer certain what their original context had been.

"The Kingdom of Heaven"

One of the most puzzling expressions frequently recurring in the Synoptic Gospels is the use of the phrase, "Kingdom of heaven" in Matthew, appearing as "Kingdom of God" in Mark and Luke. The Jewish reticence in using the name of God is more evident in "kingdom of heaven," which more likely approximates the exact expression from the mouth of Jesus.

The confusion, of course, can occur in parables such as the mustard seed—how can the kingdom of heaven grow in this way? How can the kingdom of heaven have good and bad fish in it, or counterfeit weeds?

Evidently, the reference to "heaven" has little to do with the sense of eternal reward, or for that matter, with a temporal interpretation as if Jesus was to proclaim a worldly kingdom against the Romans. Instead, "kingdom of heaven" actually represents a condition on earth in which, ideally speaking, the will of God is to be carried out perfectly. But the ideal does not exist, certainly not in this world. Hence, even while the condition should be present for the proper service of God, less than ideal situations will perforce be tolerated in the "kingdom" on earth until such time as a final cleansing and final purification.

"lest they should be converted. . . ."

READ: Matthew 13, 10-15; Mark 4, 10-12; Isaiah 6, 9-10.

Earlier in these pages, we mentioned this phrase from Isaiah, which recurs in the gospels with reference to the obscurity of the parabolic teaching of Jesus. The problem involves an apparent injustice on the part of God, whereby persons of good will would automatically be locked out of salvation by an apparent whim on the part of God.

We repeat here that these words must not be understood as some sort of harsh predestination to reprobation. "Actually, they are a sort of 'Semitism,' a Hebraic way of speaking whereby man's resulting action is pictured as if God had determined it in advance, independently of man's free will." Our way of thinking would look on man's refusal to hear God as a result of his free will. The biblical way of thinking would look on this refusal as if it had been brought about by God's all-powerful purpose, on the grounds that nothing can be beyond God's control.

It is generally agreed that Jesus had to preach his ministry within an extremely dangerous atmosphere. The religious revolution connoted by the coming of the Anointed One was only too easily connected in the popular mind with a secular revolution against the hated Romans. Thus, Jesus had to use veiled methods to gradually and safely teach the doctrine of his spiritual kingdom. The parables gave him one such opportunity.

Another means which he employed was the frequent use of the term, "Son of man," to refer to himself. This could be taken in a truly messianic sense, but lacking all the dangers of claims to secular revolution.

In no case then was the slightest injustice done to the listeners of Jesus. The degree of their sincerity was to be the measure of their success in accepting the spiritual nature of Christ's kingdom.

THE SOWER AND HIS SEED

READ: Matthew 13, 1-9; Matthew 13, 18-23; Mark 4, 1-9; Mark 4, 13-20; Luke 8, 4-8; Luke 8, 11-15

The parable of the sower is the most important of Jesus' parables of the kingdom. It certainly shows forth the typical characteristics of such stories: It does not deal with "a sower," but with "the sower," so typical is it to be. Again, it does not enter into judgment on the carelessness of a farmer who would scatter his seed so prodigally and thoughtlessly over unfruitful portions of his field. Also, the story is out of touch with actual harvest conditions: a harvest ranging to a stupendous hundredfold would be an unbelievably high return for the agricultural conditions of the time. Nor could we interpret this as reflecting fault on the part of the sower of God's word—God Himself!

A particularly interesting facet in the interpretation of this parable is the accepted opinion that the explanation of its meaning does not come from the mouth of Jesus, but was an insertion by early Church tradition, when the story was told as a sort of catechesis. However, even this explanation must hinge on the remembrance of an even earlier explanation by Jesus.

We can learn a lesson for ourselves from the history of interpretation how *not* to glean lessons from the parables of Jesus. Some writers in the past actually deduced that the parable taught that the greater part of the human race—three-fourths!—lost their souls because as much as three-fourths of the seed was lost!

THE WEEDS

READ: Matthew 13, 24-30, and 36-43

This is variously called the parable of the cockle, the tares, or the darnel weed. It concentrates on the heart of its lesson: there is the presence of bad seed (sinners) in the kingdom, this will be tolerated by God for the time being, and then final retribution will occur. Notice, however, how the parable passes over in silence the possible negligence of the slaves in leaving the field unguarded against the enemy. These servants in the story actually are merely literary foils to act as a mirror for the master's plan to reveal itself.

THE MUSTARD SEED—THE LEAVEN—THE TREASURE—THE PEARL OF GREAT PRICE

READ: Matthew 13, 31-32; Mark 4, 30-32; Matthew 13, 33; Luke 13, 20-21; Matthew 13, 44; Matthew 13, 45-46.

The one common element in these condensed parables is the element of great value connected with something otherwise very small. One item of interest concerns the domestic custom of raising bread before baking. The leaven was prepared at home by the housewife, since she saved a small portion of dough from each day's baking, or else permitted the dough to sour.

THE PRUDENT HOUSEHOLDER

Matthew 13, 52

This single sentence of Jesus, for all its shortness, has been the occasion for inversely proportionate confusion and obscurity. How can a "teacher" or "scribe" trained in the kingdom of heaven be like the master of a family bringing out from his storehouse new things and old? The sentence is in fact a compressed parable to emphasize that all the good news of the new kingdom should be merged with all the good of the law that went before it. The parable states in different words what Jesus said in the sermon on the Mount: "I have come not to abolish, but to fulfill." (Matthew 5, 17)

THE GOOD SAMARITAN

Luke 10, 30-37

The parable of the Good Samaritan has been acclaimed with so many superlatives in all centuries that one wonders whether or how any further comment can be made worthy of the original narrative. It is another example where Jesus answers a question with a story. The question was, "And who is my neighbor?" The story indicated the meaning of true neighborly charity, even to one of a hostile nationality. As a typical parable, the theme forgets about all details except its main lesson. It does not bother itself to ask: Were the robbers caught? Did the innkeeper fulfill his part of the bargain? Did the good Samaritan return to pay what was still owing? Did the man recover? Such questions were inconsequential.

THE PRODIGAL SON

Luke 15, 11-32

Two rather common misunderstandings exist concerning this parable.

The first is the impression that "prodigal" means "repentant," instead of "wasteful." The second is the impression that the parable teaches mainly the mercy of the father (God) toward the erring son (the sinner). The fact of the matter appears to be otherwise: The main lesson is for the self-righteous not to condemn nor to be jealous of their brethren who have returned to God.

THE SHREWD MANAGER

Luke 16, 1-9

No parable of Jesus has been the occasion for so much misunderstanding, confusion, and even scandal as this story of the shrewd manager. We have deliberately adopted this title in preference to other and older descriptions because it is suggested by the parable itself. Other titles in the course of history have been the traditional "unjust steward," the "unscrupulous" or "defrauding" manager. Some ancient writers even went so far as to counsel silence about the story, as if Jesus were praising sinful conduct and holding it up for imitation. No real difficulty exists if the purpose of the parable is kept in mind.

The overseer or steward or manager (call him what you will) remits a certain amount from the bills of his tenant farmers, so that after he is dismissed from his position, they will remember his "generosity." In past interpretation, some commentators thought that the manager was giving away property that rightfully belonged to his owner. A modern interpretation which places the story in its proper historical setting explains what really happened. Like every typical overseer, this rascal exacted a certain percentage of graft beyond what was due the owner of the lands. What the manager "forgave" was the graft—and there precisely lay his cleverness. The master is described by Jesus as implicitly not much better than the manager he is dismissing, for the master marvels at the ruse which gave up what had never belonged to the rascal in the first place.

Where most of the confusion occurred in the past was in a common English translation that the "lord" commended the manager for his cleverness in landing right side up. The "lord" in question, however, should have been understood as the lord of the manor, not the Lord Jesus Christ.

The closing sentence of the parable, however, seems to have capped all earlier elements for being confusing, being given as the lesson from Jesus' own lips. It has appeared in various forms in various translations, as scholars wrestled with it to make it intelligible: "Make friends by means of the unrighteous mammon, so that when it (or you) shall fail, they may receive you into everlasting dwellings." A further question exists whether the sentence should actually cap the parable, or whether it should be set apart as a distinct statement of Jesus.

We suggest an approach from the pen of the late James Kleist many years ago, "Money is a worthless thing; but use it to make friends for yourselves, so that when it gives out, they may receive you in the everlasting homes." Thus, God and mammon (from the Aramaic word for money) cannot be served simultaneously. Money should be used wisely, to build up spiritual riches from giving alms to the poor and doing other good works.

THE PHARISEE AND THE TAX GATHERER (PUBLICAN)

Luke 18, 9-14

There has always existed some doubt as to the precise lesson of this parable, whether it is to teach humility or the proper attitude toward prayer. Actually, the two merge into one, and develop from the words of Luke, "He told this parable to some who were confident of their own righteousness and despised all others."

It has always been an easy task for pharisees of later centuries to cudgel the Pharisee of the parable, not seeing themselves (and ourselves!) mirrored in the same picture. Certainly, Jesus did not condemn all Pharisees. He spoke against an observance of the law down to the smallest letter wherein all the spirit of the observance had been lost; he could not have discouraged the performance of good works and prayer, since he himself gave the good example in this regard.

It is striking that the parable does not condemn the Pharisee for the good deeds he has performed. The good deeds are truly far more than was required, and Jesus does not blame him for this. It is the implicit attitude of the prayer which is at fault, namely, a reminder to God of the individual virtues, self-centered rather than God-centered.

The Aramaic idiom is behind the more correct phrase that "this man went back to his house justified more than the other," instead of "justified rather than the other."

The parable ends with another of the proverbial comments which afford occasion for conflicting interpretation: "Everyone who exalts himself shall be humiliated; but he who humbles himself shall be exalted." It remains an open question whether this phrase belongs to the parable as an integral conclusion and summing up, or whether it is a sort of appendix that adds to the parable while independent of it.

We occidental moderns can easily miss the master stroke in . choice of the publican as the counterfoil of the Pharisee. As far as public appearances or opinion were concerned, the tax gatherer was a renegade Jew, hired by the hated Romans, and loathed for the unjust extortions he had committed. Yet in the parable, he is pitted against the very personification of the full external observance of the sacred law.

It has been said that Shakespeare's *Merchant of Venice* artfully attacked the self-righteous vengeance of Christians on Jews, while appearing to condemn the miserliness of Shylock. So, too, in this parable of the Pharisee and the publican, Jesus may well have put all of us in the uncomfortable position of considering ourselves the humble publican while we scathingly denounce the apparently proud Pharisee, never seeing ourselves in the picture.

THE CAPRICIOUS CHILDREN

Luke 7, 31-35; Matthew 11, 16-19

Our reason for selecting this parable from the many possibilities in the gospels stems from the human interest involved. The context gives us an otherwise unknown sidelight on the character of Jesus, on his everyday actions, and on the way his methods were accepted by his contemporaries. The comparison is very clear: John the Baptist was rejected because John was too ascetical; but Jesus now is rejected on the grounds that Jesus is too "worldly," a "glutton," a "wine guzzler"! Like children whose whims change from moment to moment and cannot agree on the rules of the games they are playing, so have the people rejected Jesus and his message for any flimsy pretext, "damning him if he does, and damning him if he doesn't."

THE MERCILESS DEBTOR

Matthew 18, 23-35

Someone has said that this parable teaches the same lesson as the Lord's prayer, on the forgiveness of our debtors; but pray God that God does not take us at our word and forgive us merely as far as we forgive our debtors!

To get some idea of the difference between the two debts mentioned in the parable, the sum forgiven by the king is about 600,000 times as large as the amount owed by the fellow-servant.

THE LABORERS IN THE VINEYARD

Matthew 19, 30; 20, 1-16

The first point to note is that the phrase, "Many are called but few are

.ot belong as the conclusion to this parable. Scholars are . rightly ends the parable of the wedding feast (which

.tory of the interpretation of this parable continues the lessons .n how not to interpret the parables of Jesus! Ancient commentat. in flagrant disregard for the type of literature under discussion, actually considered the first-hour workers as Jews, the eleventh-hour workers as gentiles; or else they broke up the centuries according to arbitrary whims, consigning friends or enemies to whatever hour they wished, according to the century or the country where these people lived.

The one genuine lesson is that God is free to distribute His gifts as He sees fit. The beggar who receives a million dollars has no right to complain that another beggar received two million.

The parable has come in for some unfortunate modern misapplication in the area of labor relations. On the false premise that Jesus is praising the tactic of making "all that the trade can bear," one might wrongly conclude that all payments are fair in situations where persons are in no position to bargain for their just due, but must take what is offered, right or not.

But the parable was not uttered in the context of labor relations. The economic condition it presents appears only as the foil for the lesson of God's generosity in giving His gifts as He sees fit in His all-perfect love and goodness.

THE GREAT BANQUET—THE WEDDING BANQUET—THE GUEST WITHOUT A WEDDING GARMENT

READ: Luke 14, 15-24; Matthew 22, 1-10; Matthew 22, 11-14

The question arises whether the parable in Luke is the same as that in Matthew, with a different meaning and a different emphasis; or whether it is separate and distinct of itself. Jesus must have frequently used this comparison of the kingdom of God as a great banquet. We suggest here the opinion that Luke's parable stands by itself.

a) As for the common theme of a banquet, this in itself would not argue to identity, precisely because a banquet was so logical to use as a setting for the kingdom of God. Jesus would be logical in using the comparison more than once.

b) This banquet in Luke is a supper given by an unnamed man. In Matthew it is a wedding feast given by a king for his son.

c) In Luke no violence is done to the single servant reminding the future guests. In Matthew the many servants given this task are maltreated and murdered.

d) The lesson in Luke seems to be restricted to extending the message of the kingdom to the ordinary Jews after the message had been rejected by the leaders. In Matthew the lesson strongly emphasizes the rejection of God's message from the prophets. The supplanting of the Jews by the gentiles in the kingdom is implied.

e) Matthew adds to his main narrative a second and completely independent unit, the guest without the wedding garment. There does not seem to be room for this development of thought in the parable of Luke.

f) We admit that Matthew's gospel usually presents the discourses of Jesus within a topical rather than a chronological framework. Hence, the time when the parable of the wedding feast was uttered cannot be determined too precisely. Nor can it be determined whether it was used once, or many times. None the less, since it logically fits with the other parables in Matthew appearing in the closing days of Jesus' life, the story of the wedding feast seems to have been given much later than the parable of the great banquet, which Luke presents apparently earlier in the public ministry of Jesus.

The passage of the guest without the wedding garment provides an additional enigma. There is good reason to hold that this is a fragment of another parable, and that it was fused with the story of the wedding feast. By whom was this done? One theory proposes that the Matthean tradition itself combined the parable of the feast with another banquet parable in which the wedding-garment motif was prominent, since their settings were the same.

It would seem more likely, however, that Jesus himself was responsible for the combination. We know how Jesus presented the kingdom under the literary figure of a banquet. In this he built upon the Jewish tradition concerning the messianic banquet when the anointed of the Lord would come in his glory. The parable as Jesus used it was a facile vehicle capable of all sorts of adaptations. A kind of literary economy on the part of Jesus could have employed the already established setting to inculcate the need for the proper dispositions in belonging to the kingdom.

Again, we can learn from the mistakes of the past how not to interpret gospel passages outside their original context of time and place. The ancient etiquette would be reflected in that the king came in to look at the guests; he would not himself eat with them. The breach of good manners when the ceremonial robe was lacking would be a great insult. The king's question is rather quite gentle, "My good fellow, how did you get in here thus?" It is certainly not a case of condemnation without the case having been heard. The speechlessness of the man increases rather than diminishes the insult.

Writers of more insular centuries attempted to relieve the appearance of ruthless injustice by inventing strategems from their own day and age, but all in vain! The host supposedly provided such robes, and the man failed to make use of the service; or in the rush of being invited from the by-ways, without advance notice there was no time to become properly vested!

The one point of the parable is that a gross insult was done to the king. Hence, the punishment is equally severe, and the words of Jesus move from the figurative language of the parable and merge into the lesson of "exterior darkness" implying deliberate unforgiven sin.

Because of the many possibilities for misunderstanding the parable's final phrase, "Many are called, but few are chosen," we should first determine what it does *not* mean. We are safe in excluding it as a direct reference made by Jesus to indicate the number of the damned or the number of the saved.

Jesus was repeatedly asked by his listeners about the number of the saved, but he never gave them a direct answer (as in the reference to entering by the narrow door in Luke 13, 24). The entrance was narrow in the sense Jesus means: self-renunciation is necessary.

Moreover, Jesus' evasiveness on this subject is all the more remarkable in view of the prevalent tradition in Jewish literature of his time that very few would be saved. It would have been very easy for him to go along with the popular belief, but Jesus refused either to agree or to disagree with it. Instead, he reiterated the need for a personal effort to save one's soul, with no need to satisfy the speculative curiousity that would be of no profit to one's own salvation. The subject was a mystery to be concealed in the infinite wisdom and love of God.

No argument can be solidly deduced from the use of the word "Many," since the fact is that *all* are called to salvation by God, not merely "many." At the same time, if we were to argue from the other direction, we would have to admit that "many" is often used in the New Testament in the sense of "all," as in the words of Jesus at the Last Supper, that the blood of Jesus will be shed for "many"—actually all.

But ultimately we must conclude that "few" and "many" are terms so relative that one cannot deduce from Jesus' words any conclusion regarding salvation. In any event, the example has its value to show how diametrically opposite meaning can be obtained by juggling scripture texts, if one wishes to do so.

All this, however, does not reach the root of what the "many are called" phrase possibly means. It evidently refers neither to the wedding feast nor to the wedding-garment episode but is a general truth that can sum up the gist of both parables. It teaches in a very strong way that all members of the human race are called by God. Those who are not chosen are rejected because of their bad will. The "few chosen" phrase acts as a strong paradox to the "many called." Not all of the "many" follow their lights to enter the kingdom, whether they be among the Jews first invited or among the later gentiles in the kingdom of Christ.

THE NARROW DOOR

READ: Luke 13, 22-30

This parable resembles the words of Jesus in Matthew (7, 13-14) concerning the narrow door to salvation. It differs, however, in that it applies primarily to acceptance of Jesus' kingdom instead of referring to salvation for all. Notice how the stage is set with the explicit question of a disciple, whether few are saved. The evasiveness of Jesus is deliberate, countering with the call to self-renunciation.

THE TEN VIRGINS (or THE TEN MAIDENS)

READ: Matthew 25, 1-13

The details of this parable afford an occasion to summarize marriage customs in the times of Jesus, even though according to parabolic license, some parts of the story do not agree fully with that experience.

The "ten virgins" or "ten maidens" are bridesmaids in modern parlance. "Ten" in itself has no particular significance, and was evidently chosen as a round number.

The ceremony involved is that of the wedding, closing the year of espousal, when the bridegroom would solemnize his marriage—espousal by coming to get his bride at her home. He would be accompanied by his male friends, who in the archaic phrase of a long discarded translation were rather mistakenly called "children of the bridegroom." These wedding celebrations would begin in the late afternoon and evening and might last the whole night through, if not for several days.

For the purposes of the lesson of the parable, the bridesmaids hold only small clay lamps, which would soon exhaust their oil supply. If they had had torches, which were also customary, the situation of the parable could not have occurred. On several other counts, too, Jesus tailored his parable to fit the lesson he desired. Thus, when the five improvident girls are told to go to the shopkeepers to buy more oil, the fact is that the shops would hardly be open in the middle of the night.

Suddenly, the narrative moves into its lesson, while not completely deserting the story of the wedding. The doors of the groom's house are now locked against the late-comers, and this is hardly a feature of a true wedding. No longer is the groom "who knows them not" the earthly bridegroom but the eternal Lord and Master, Jesus himself. The careful watching for the bridegroom is a clear harkening to the Old Testament theme that Israel is the bride of God her spouse.

Again, we can learn from historical mistakes how not to read meanings into parables which are not present. Because the bridesmaids slept while waiting for the wedding party, some ancient commentators saw the need to condemn spiritual sloth! None the less, the girls with the oil slept just as much as did those who ran short! The worldly wisdom of refusing to share one's abundance (of oil, in this case) with those less fortunate also came in for its share of criticism.

The one true lesson is evidently a warning to be ready for God's call, whenever it comes.

THE TALENTS and THE GOLD PIECES

READ: Matthew 25, 14-30; Luke 19, 12-27

Again we have two separate parables, with an identical lesson: God's gifts, whether natural or supernatural, should be used properly. However, the many similarities in the two narratives again suggest the possibility that there was originally one story which later appeared with varying details. None the less, the differences are so marked and the occasions on which the parables were uttered are evidently so far removed that we can conclude that Jesus used the same literary framework on at least two different occasions in different ways to teach the same lesson.

In Matthew's account, a man who goes abroad entrusts his property to three servants, to the amount of ten talents, five, and one. The talent in question was at one time considered a sum worth at least $1,200—before inflation! The servants are to trade with their master's money and to return a profit.

The man who received the single talent has unprofitably hidden the talent in the ground and thus receives the condemnation as being a wicked and lazy slave. The paradoxical proverb itself is difficult to explain on every score: "For to every one who possesses, more shall be given, and he shall have abundance; but from whom who does not possess, even that which he has shall be taken away." Actually, this is but another way of emphasizing the genuine largesse of the master, who does not keep the single unused talent for himself but adds it to the ten won by the energetic slave.

Why should the third man be called wicked and lazy? In one respect, he merely tries to manufacture an alibi for his laziness in not trading with the money. The pretext he resorts to only makes his case look worse, for he gives an insolent caricature of his master.

The useless slave is therefore cast into outer darkness. Again, Jesus uses certain phrases here which leave the realm of the story and merge into questions of the judgment of God.

In the parable told by Luke, another thread appears in the story. This is the reference to a nobleman receiving a kingdom. It was apparently prompted by the fact that some of Jesus' listeners supposed that the kingdom of God would make its appearance at once. Jesus accordingly tells of a nobleman who travels to a distant country to receive a kingdom for himself.

This was a manifest allusion to the custom of princes of the Herodian dynasty to travel to Rome to receive their kingdom from the hands of the emperor. The allusion is all the more clear when Jesus mentions that the nobleman's "countrymen hated him, so they sent an embassy after him with the petition, 'We are not willing that this person should reign over us.' " Such was the embassy sent to Rome by the Jews in a fruitless attempt to prevent Archelaus from succeeding his father Herod in 4 B.C.

To follow up for ourselves this particular motif to the end, Jesus concludes the parable in the nobleman's words, "As for those enemies of mine who did not wish me to reign over them, bring them here, and execute them in my presence." Jesus is certainly not comparing his kingdom to the petty states of the tyrannical Herodian families, nor could he even suggest a parallel between his holiness and the bestiality of men like Herod the Great, Archelaus, or Herod Antipas. The heart of the comparison simply points out that his kingdom will not come at once, and until Christ the king returns in the glory of his kingdom, his servants should profitably use the gifts God has given them. When he does come, he will crush the enemies whose machinations he tolerated to exist before his arrival.

Such then is the context within which Luke's parable of the gold pieces fits. The nobleman calls ten servants and gives each of them one gold piece, a *mna* once worth twenty dollars. In only three cases do we hear what happens. The largesse appears typical of hyperbole in the parable: namely, the reward of cities for trafficking profitably, something otherwise out of reasonable proportion. The third slave, speaking like the unprofitable servant of Matthew, implicitly reproaches his master for miserliness by means of the excuse of hiding the gold piece in his napkin. The paradoxical proverb occurs again, emphasizing as it did in Matthew, the generosity of the master, who heaps rewards on those who have been faithful to his commands.

JESUS THE VINE

READ: John 15, 1-11

There is little difficulty in understanding the words of Jesus here. The one reason we mention the passage is to give an example of an extended parable which fits so many details that it has more often been called an allegory than a parable. It presents a tremendously powerful lesson that theologically all grace comes to us through Jesus the Savior.

COMPRESSED PARABLES

"PHYSICIAN, CURE THYSELF!"

READ: Luke 4, 23

There exists a large group of sayings of Jesus which in themselves do not constitute parables in the usual sense of the word, but which impart their teaching by way of a verbal comparison. It is possible that they were first delivered by Jesus in longer form and later compressed into summaries by the gospel tradition. The paradox occurs in some cases that these short parabolic sayings can cause more difficulty and lengthier explanation than their brevity implies.

The current example has its particular interest in that it is a proverb Jesus quotes when his fellow Nazarenes demand miracles such as they had heard were done at Capernaum. The proverb was implicitly first in the mouths of his countrymen; Jesus answered them with another proverb that no prophet is acceptable in his own country. The meaning of the Nazarenes was equivalent to saying, "If you cannot work miracles here, you are like a physician unable to cure himself and members of his own family." The retort of Jesus was another way of saying, "Familiarity breeds contempt."

THE SALT

READ: Matthew 5, 13; Mark 9, 49-50; Luke 14, 34-35.

This compressed metaphor has more often been misapplied historically than understood in its correct gospel context. It does not have the connotation that "salt of the earth" is something most precious; salt was common enough. Instead, Jesus reminded the disciples that they had the duty of spreading the preservative influence of Christian doctrine. Just as salt preserves food from corruption, so were they to preserve the world from corrupt doctrine. The "salt that becomes insipid" was a reference to the many impurities in Palestinian salt obtained from evaporating water from the Dead Sea. These impurities made it easily deliquescent, a viscuous mass considered useless. The added reference in Mark (9, 50) whereby salt symbolizes friendship was based on the seasoning properties of salt, especially at a common meal of good fellowship.

THE LAMP ON THE LAMPSTAND; THE CITY ON THE MOUNTAIN

READ: Matthew 5, 14-15; Mark 4, 21

The common element in these comparisons emphasizes the responsibility of the disciples to give good example to the world around them, like a prominent light and a prominent city.

THE EYE THE LAMP OF THE BODY

READ: Matthew 6, 22-23; Luke 11, 34-36

This compressed parable tends to be misunderstood by moderns who think of the eye as an organ to receive light rather than to give light. The thought of Jesus, however, does not think in so "scientific" a mold. The meaning here is that just as the eye, like a lamp, guides the body properly, so should the sound mind (the "heart") direct one's life with proper singleness of purpose.

PEARLS BEFORE SWINE

READ: Matthew 7, 6

Few sayings of Jesus have become part of our language more than this comparison. The general meaning of the admonition is a warning not to profane sacred things. However, a literary problem exists because the proper parallelism seems to have been changed: "holy—dogs; pearls—swine." The thought is so Semitic that many scholars look with favor on a theory which reconstructs the meaning of the word "holy." In Aramaic this word so closely resembles "rings" (of gold) that it may have been translated by mistake into its present form. The original reading would then be, "Do not give your gold rings to dogs nor throw your pearl necklaces before swine."

AS THE TREE, SO THE FRUIT

READ: Matthew 7, 16-20; Matthew 12, 33; Luke 6, 43-45

Jesus evidently used the comparison of trees and their fruits on more than one occasion. The idea, however, is the same: good effects can come only from good causes. The condensed parable has come in for its share of misunderstanding on the score that a healthy tree often enough produces a certain percentage of rotten fruit. The objection fails to note the comparison, which is the point of the parable. The parable is interested in the kind of fruit, not the amount of healthy fruit, and should not be pushed illogically to an unintended extreme.

THE OLD AND THE NEW

READ: Matthew 9, 16-17; Mark 2, 21-22; Luke 5, 36-39

The exact meaning of these parabolic comparisons is open to discussion, but the general meaning is certain: Jesus is teaching the radical newness (that is, "new from the roots") of the doctrine of the kingdom. Yet we must remember that we must not push this interpretation so far as to negate the other words of Jesus that he has come not to abolish but to fulfill the law. The examples are taken from everyday experience which the audience would readily understand. A strong and shrinking patch will merely rip the old cloth and make the rent larger. New, fermenting wine will burst goatskin "bottles" that have already been weakened from fermentation of earlier wine. New goatskins that are strong should be used for new fermentation.

THE GREAT HARVEST

READ: Matthew 9, 37-38; Luke 10, 2

The justifiable conclusion from the words of Jesus concerning the need for laborers in the harvest is that much good can be done if only the human instruments are available. Historically, this parabolic saying was misinterpreted as if it meant that most of the human race would be lost to salvation because not enough laborers were working for souls. The answer must always be that the question of eternal salvation rests in the inscrutable loving wisdom of God. In any event, it is not the point of this compressed parable.

Nor should the parable be pressed so far as to imply that the doctrine of Jesus would successfully win over all souls if only there are enough evangelists. Other factors are present, to control such an event. "Success" in the apostolate does not ultimately depend on the work of the evangelists. The greatest proof is the fact that Jesus himself, incarnate holiness and wisdom, did not "succeed' in the apostolate of his lifetime.

CRUMBS FOR THE DOGS

Matthew 15, 26-27; Mark 7, 27-28

These sentences have often been pointed out as some of the most delightful bits of repartee in the gospels. The scene was the pagan districts north of Palestine, where Jesus appears to repulse the Canaanite woman, as if the Chosen People were alone to receive the benefits of Jesus' teaching and miracles. That Jesus was not acting harshly is evident from the continuing insistence of the woman, who evidently feels she is receiving encouragement to make her point more strongly. Her faith is so strong that she can ask for the "crumbs" of God's grace which are left over from the "table" of those who appear to be given preference.

THE BODY AND THE EAGLES (vultures)

READ: Matthew 24, 28; Luke, 17, 37

The surprising reaction to this compressed parable is that persons who do not come from a rural environment are unacquainted with the habits of birds of prey. The meaning is, "Just as the presence of vultures in the air tells you that carrion lies beneath them, so the signs will tell you what is coming"—in this case, the fall of Jerusalem.

THE MYSTERIOUS WIND

READ: John 3, 8

This succinct comparison has the rather rare quality of keeping its ambiguity in various languages. The reason is that the word for "spirit" is so often identical with or close to the word for "wind." The spirit of God works in souls gently, quietly, effectively. His action is like that of the wind, which we do not see but whose action we hear. The Latin *spiritus,* like the Hebrew *ruah,* both mean "spirit" and "wind."

THE IDENTITY OF THE ANONYMOUS PENITENT WOMAN—MARY MAGDALEN?

READ: Luke 7, 36-50; Luke 8, 2-3; Matthew 26, 6-13; Mark 14, 3-9; John 12, 1-8; John 11, 1-2

We come now to an interesting question whose interpretation has influenced even our everyday language, where a "magdalen" is defined in the dictionary as a reformed prostitute. In the gospel passages listed above, there are certainly three sets of stories; the question historically has been whether these stories refer to one, two, or three women: Here are the three literary figures visible in the gospels:

1) An anonymous penitent prostitute;

2) Mary from Bethany, who was the sister of Martha and Lazarus;

3) Mary from Magdala, a town in Galilee, who was with Jesus on Calvary and after his resurrection.

We present the opinion here that these are really three different persons. Such was the view held by writers of the church in the East. The opposite view which identified them as one person was more prevalent in the West since the time of Gregory the Great in the sixth century.

Whether the question can ever be definitely settled is a moot point. The common opinion of biblical scholars today is that no evidence exists in the gospels to support the contention that one woman appears several times with different names, or that more than one woman was a great and publicly known sinner.

Why were these three thought to be the same person? The confusion arose from an application of the mathematical statement, "Two things equal to a third thing are equal to each other." In this case:

1) Mary of Bethany was supposed to be another name for Mary of Magdala.

2) The banquet at the house of Simon the Pharisee was supposed to be the same as the banquet of Simon the leper.

3) Because one woman—the reformed prostitute—wept when she anointed Jesus with perfume as a sign of her repentance, this was thought to be the same action as when another woman—Mary of Bethany—anointed Jesus (with no weeping) as a sign of honor to him.

4) The anonymous woman in Matthew (26) and Mark (14) was thought to be the same as the anonymous woman in Luke (7), both of whom anointed Jesus but under different circumstances.

5) The fact that Mary Magdalen had been freed from the influence of "seven demons" was thought to mean that she was the devil's slave in sin.

We should emphasize that Bethany in Judea (the home of one Mary) is at least a hundred miles south of Magdala on the shores of the Lake of Galilee (the home of another Mary). The time of the banquet in Luke is evidently during the public ministry of Jesus, while the time of the banquet at the home of Martha and Lazarus was shortly before the apprehension and passion of Jesus. Likewise, when Luke completes what we call his chapter 7 with the story of the reformed anonymous prostitute, he begins our chapter 8 with a reference to Mary of Magdala as if she were being introduced to the narrative for the first time.

Hence, we conclude that the repentant woman whose dramatic interruption of Simon (the Pharisee's) banquet was the occasion for the parable of the two debtors should not be identified as Mary of Magdala, and much less as Mary of Bethany. She should remain in the anonymity Luke mercifully decided to bestow upon her.

THE ESCHATOLOGICAL DISCOURSE

READ: Matthew 24, 1-51; Mark 13, 1-37; Luke 21, 5-36

In reading these passages, you should keep in mind that they represent probably the most difficult topic of all gospel commentaries. The various interpretations that have been presented are almost as individual as the persons originating them. That is why what we offer here can make no pretence at being the last word on the subject or the definitive answer to the many questions that arise. Some principles, however, can be listed as relatively certain:

a) The lengthy discourse as we have it now is the result of marked editing. It is possible that some of the words of Jesus in this discourse were uttered at different times and in different contexts, but there seems to be no way to determine certainly how these can be sifted out and classified.

b) The discourse is highly colored by thought and wording that is called "apocalyptic." The apocalyptic literary form is foreign to us moderns, but to ancient biblical writers and readers it made sense. It is characterized by highly figurative language, it tends to compress the time of events of this life compared to the time of the end of the world, and it would refer to fire, storms, and phenomena of nature as symbols of God's power. It also abounds in prophetic hyperbole.

c) The wording which we find confusing in our day seems to have caused parallel confusion even in the times of the early Christian church. We have to recall that in those early generations after the death and resurrection of Jesus the belief was prevalent that the end of the world was at hand, since Jesus the Messiah had come.

The "eschatological discourse" gets its name from the Greek *ta eschata* (pronounced es'-ka-ta), meaning "the last things." The discourse as such would appear to have been given by Jesus in the days directly preceding his arrest and condemnation to death.

We must remember that the disciples first asked Jesus two distinct questions, which in their minds evidently were two aspects of the same event: "Tell us, when shall these things be?" (that is, the destruction of the temple at Jerusalem, as prophesied by Christ); and "What shall be the sign of thy coming and of the end of the world?" For the disciples the destruction of the temple would be equivalent to saying that the world had come to its end.

Jesus' answer appears to fall into distinct parts according to the two questions. In some cases we have little difficulty in recognizing what pertains to each part, and where. For example, tribulation for the apostles, the appearance of false prophets, the temple's profanation (the "abomination of desolation"), the haste to leave the city without stopping for belongings or clothes—these and similar details seem to hold true as signs of the impending capture of Jerusalem as it did occur in 70 A.D. Jesus' further words that such tribulation "has not been since the beginning of the world until now, nor shall ever be," can be understood as prophetic foreshortening or hyperbole, a strong and exaggerated way of pointing out the suffering which would happen. They are not, in such an interpretation, taken as a strict comparison.

The second part of Jesus' discourse refers to the darkening of the sun and moon and the gathering of mankind by the angels (messengers) of the Son of Man. Even the phrase, "immediately after the affliction of those earlier days," does not cause the difficulty it seems to have at first sight, for in such prophetical foreshortening everything is seen as happening at once. The interval between the fall of Jerusalem and the end of the world is passed over in silence.

The discourse has sometimes been broken up into a general outline thus:

1) Signs of the fall of Jerusalem;
2) Signs of the end of the world;
3) Time of the fall of Jerusalem;
4) Time of the end of the world.

Thus, the phrase that "this generation will not pass away" would refer to the fall of Jerusalem. According to this outlook, it was fulfilled, for "all these things" concerning the fall of Jerusalem were truly accomplished forty years later.

On the other hand, when Jesus added, "Of that day and hour, no one knows. . . . none but the Father alone," he was referring to the second event, the end of the world.

What of the phrase, "Heaven and earth shall pass away"? This is a vigorous and colorful Hebrewism, "Even if the heavens and the earth were to pass away, my words shall not pass away."

You should note in particular that the difficulty of interpreting the meaning of these words of Jesus must have been present at a very early stage in the infant church. Both Matthew (24, 15) and Mark (13, 14) repeat the phrase, "Let him who reads, understand!"

We should admit candidly that even our separation of the definite and clearly described material from the vague future date and symbolic language does not remove all the difficulties in the eschatological discourse, but we can at least discern that the fall of Jerusalem can be looked on as a symbol of the end of the world, when God's final judgment will come.

READINGS IN JOHN

READ: John 1, 1-18 (and as much of John as possible)

You can easily notice the difference in style in this theological prologue compared with the style of the rest of the gospel. In the nineteenth century, many scriptural scholars were accepting the theory that John's gospel must have borrowed the ideas of "word," "light," "darkness," and other abstract terms from Greek philosophy. Such a theory denied that John's gospel came close to the time of Jesus. Fortunately, the discovery from 1947 onward of the Dead Sea Scrolls from Qumran and the Murabba'at has proven that the use of terms like these was indeed known at the time of Jesus.

JOHN 2—The Wedding feast at Cana

This event represented the final ceremony for marriage: the end of the espousal period, when the bridegroom took the bride into his own home.

We should mention at this time that all scripture scholars point out the great symbolism which exists in the gospel of John. The special element to note, however, is that the existence of this symbolism should not be interpreted to rule out the historical event behind it. John sees symbolism in history; we moderns should not destroy the historical by exaggerating the symbolism in John.

JOHN 3—Nicodemus

Here we should mention another characteristic of John's gospel: the reflections on the words of Jesus, which carry his thought farther, and which often are so continuous with his thought that it is difficult to determine with certainty where the words of Jesus end, and where the words of the reflection begin. A typical example occurs in 3, 16: "For God so loved the world that he gave his only-begotten son, that those who believe in him may not perish, but may have life everlasting."

JOHN 4

In the story of Jesus and the Samaritan woman at the well, we meet still another characteristic of John's gospel. In a dialogue with Jesus, the questions from the other speaker often take the words of Jesus in one sense in order to give him the opportunity to make a correction and indicate exactly what he means. In this fourth chapter of John, such an example would be the question of the woman (4, 11): "Sir, from where do you have this living water?"

JOHN 5

A very celebrated instance of the value of archeological discoveries is connected with this chapter. Earlier scholars tended to dismiss this chapter as mere symbolism, and they pointed to the reference to the "pool with five porches," asking how any pool could have five (instead of four) porches. Excavations near the site of the former temple at Jerusalem revealed such a pool: it was actually an upper and a lower pool, and the porch or division between the two sections constituted the fifth porch. John's geographical references have elsewhere been shown again and again to agree with what we can learn today of the distances and the topography of the Palestine of Jesus.

JOHN 6

This chapter should not be skipped; it is the tremendously significant promise Jesus makes of himself as the Eucharist.

JOHN 8, 3-10

The special point to note about this passage is the generally accepted belief that originally it was not part of the gospel of John but more likely part of one of the other gospels. You can see for yourself how different it is in style and in language from the surrounding paragraphs.

JOHN 14, 15, 16, 17

These chapters containing the "farewell discourse" of Jesus to his disciples, together with his priestly prayer, have often been counted among the most sublime literature in all the world.

THE LAST SUPPER

READ: Matthew 26, 17-36; Mark 14, 12-26; Luke 22, 7-30; John 13

The narratives of the Last Supper and of the Passion and death of Jesus were evidently of such importance to the early church that they were the first collections of actions and sayings which later became our gospels. In no other part of Jesus' life are we given so much information concerning his activities. Again, the four gospels are by no means identical in their treatment of their subject; but they dovetail so often in giving added details of the sufferings of Jesus that the so-called problems in gospel interpretation are far less for us in these passages than elsewhere.

If you can be more aware of the time-sequence of these actions, you will be all the more able to understand them better and follow them with more interest. There is definitely the centuries-old "problem" as to what day of the week was the day of the Last Supper. You should first remember that Jewish custom began each day at nightfall, not at midnight. You should also remember that the Passover was the greatest feast of the year, and evidently in the year Jesus died, it coincided with the observance of the Sabbath—Saturday.

If Jesus had observed a true Passover supper with his disciples, that should have been on a Friday evening. The leaders of the people had already refused to enter the house of Pilate on Friday morning since they did not wish to defile themselves legally from eating the Passover meal that evening. None the less, we are certain from all four gospels that Jesus died on Friday some time after midday. Yet the meal which Jesus shared with his disciples has all the appearances of the ritual of the Passover supper.

All sorts of suggestions have been made throughout the centuries to explain this difficulty, some of them almost ridiculous. One such suggestion was that the Jewish leaders postponed the Passover one day so that they could conveniently put Jesus to death while they had him in their power ! The fact is, however, that common consensus put the Passover on a Friday evening, coinciding with the Sabbath, as John's gospel makes clear.

More serious suggestions have been made on the basis that Judaism was not so monolithic at the time of Christ that the feasts had to be observed at identical times, as if the Pharisaic custom might have had its Passover a day before the Sadducees.

Perhaps the most likely approach to explain the dilemma involved has come from the pen of Annie Jaubert, a French scripture scholar writing in 1957. She called attention to the calendar used at Qumran, which calculated the Passover according to the sun, instead of using the calculation by a lunar or moon calendar as at Jerusalem. In such a case, the meal Jesus had with his disciples would have been on Tuesday evening, considered a true Passover. The high priests, following the lunar calendar or "official" temple way of reckoning, would have had their Passover meal on Friday evening, as John's gospel makes clear.

Annie Jaubert's theory has much more to recommend it, in making an allowance for ample time for all the events which the gospels record as having happened to Jesus. Did you ever try to visualize the haste that would be necessary if the Last Supper ended at 9 o'clock on a Thursday evening; if the time to walk to the opposite end of the city to the garden of Gethsemani was added to the time of the agony of Jesus, evidently up to midnight; if there had to be time before dawn for Annas to hold one trial and Caiaphas one trial, and another trial at dawn; if Jesus appeared first before Pilate at dawn, thence was sent to Herod, thence back to Pilate? In between all these trials and movements through Jerusalem there would have to be enough time for Jesus to be scourged and mocked and crowned with thorns.

It certainly is not clear from the Synoptic gospels over how many hours or days the ordeal of Jesus was spread. Liturgically, the Passion is looked on as beginning on Thursday evening, but this is not a final argument when you ask yourself about a more exact calendar. The question remains open. The solution from the use of the Qumran calendar by Jesus seems more and more likely as the years go on.

In any event, the Last Supper of Jesus began at dusk. You should not visualize the apostles and Jesus as sitting upright in western fashion at one table. Instead, they reclined (as the gospels explicitly say), following the Roman custom of reclining on couches, resting on their left elbows and eating with their right. The table would most likely be horseshoe-shaped, with the diners on the outside of the horseshoe. This arrangement also explains for us how John could lean back on the breast of Jesus and ask him confidentially who was the betrayer among the apostles.

THE PASSION AND DEATH OF JESUS

READ: Matthew 26 and 27; Mark 14 and 15; Luke 22 and 23; John 18 and 19.

You may have read elsewhere that the location of the Via Dolorosa or Way of the Cross in Jerusalem is not historically that of the path which Jesus followed in his sufferings. That statement is true at least in the sense that the Jerusalem of today is ten feet or more higher than the Jerusalem of the time of Jesus.

The one location in Jerusalem which has received universal acceptance is that of Calvary—the present church of the Holy Sepulchre. Scholars are divided on the question whether the "Lithostrotos" or stone-pavement courtyard where Pilate condemned Jesus to death was near the corner of the temple (in Pilate's Fortress Antonia) or at the western gate of the city, near the palace of Herod.

You should not visualize the cross that Jesus carried as consisting of a cross-piece connected to an upright. As far as we can reconstruct the method of crucifixion, the condemned man had to carry only the cross-piece—and this would explain more easily for us how Simon of Cyrene could carry the cross of Jesus behind Jesus. At the place of crucifixion, the upright was already in the ground. The man's hands were first nailed to the cross-piece, and then he was lifted, so that the cross-piece rested in a crotch or support in the upright, when his feet were nailed to the upright.

The real cause of Jesus' death was probably asphyxiation, due to cramping of the muscles of the chest from the weight of his body as it hung from his crucified hands. The reason why the Roman soldiers broke the leg bones of the two thieves to hasten their death was precisely to bring about this death from the inability to breathe. Since Jesus was already dead, his legs were not broken. The opening of the side of Jesus occurred after he was already judged to be dead. The "blood and water" of which John speaks is evidently a mixture of blood from the right auricle of the heart (the only chamber which has blood in it after death), and serum or lymph which had been filling the lungs of Jesus because of the physical shock he had been suffering.

The remarkable trait of the four gospels which you should notice is their controlled objectivity as they relate what is the source of the greatest horror and shock to the authors of these traditions. Perhaps we ought to imitate this attitude ourselves, in recognizing that from the horror and failure of the crucifixion of Jesus, God has brought and still will bring the greatest joy and goodness possible—far more than we can ever imagine.

THE RESURRECTION

READ: Matthew 28; Mark 16; Luke 24; John 20 and 21

The resurrection narratives in the gospels stand apart from the rest of the gospels in a way you can easily see for yourself. Notice how they reflect the confusion of the early reports that "He is risen!" Details are added in one gospel or other, but the main historical fact is the empty tomb. Notice, too, that nowhere do the gospels describe the resurrection of Jesus. It is commonly taken for granted, when people read the gospels that Jesus rose from the dead on Easter Sunday morning. Strictly speaking, the gospels do not say even that. The impression Jesus rose "on the third day" comes from the words of Paul (1 Corinthians 15, 4) and from the gospel predictions of Jesus that he would rise on the third day.

This complete silence in describing the event of the resurrection of Jesus is one of the greatest if not the greatest factor in favor of the truth of the gospel stories. Theologically speaking, the resurrection of Jesus is far more than a mere revivification of a human body; it is his glorification in a way we cannot understand; and, even more, his resurrection is part of his redemption just as much as his sufferings redeemed us. None the less, although it is true that we cannot understand the resurrection because it is a mystery of faith, we can understand the fact that something happened that is far beyond our capacity to grasp, and this "something" is the object of our faith in the Risen Jesus.

As you read the various gospel stories of the resurrection, keep in mind the "traditional" arguments which doubting critics used in order to say that the resurrection never happened:

a) One approach is to deny completely all truth to the gospel stories. There is no adequate reply to this approach because it states flatly that it will never grant the existence of the resurrection of Jesus, no matter what historical evidence is brought forward.

b) Another approach was called the "coma theory," holding that Jesus never died on the cross, but that he was in the tomb in a coma. Then, when he (himself?) pushed aside the rolling stone and walked through the city, the stories of his re-appearance to his disciples later were exaggerated into the present stories of the empty tomb and the apparitions. The merit of the "coma theory" is that it at least pretends to follow the gospel account, even though it arrives at a different conclusion. Against it, if one insists on accepting gospel evidence, is the fact that the heart of Jesus was pierced after he died on the cross; that the evidence of his death was accepted not only by his friends but also by his enemies; and that the disciples do not recognize their Lord as exactly the person he was previously. In other words, the coma theory is a theory brought into existence in order to deny the resurrection, not from the internal nature of the gospel stories.

c) A less respectable theory claims that the body of Jesus was stolen after Jesus died—stolen by his friends and disciples so that they could claim he rose from the dead! Not only does this descend to the lowest depths of deception and deliberate lying; it also forgets (like the coma theory) the gospel evidence of the disbelief of the disciples. They certainly do not triumphantly parade their "risen" Lord. One variation of the "stolen body" theory even claimed that the enemies of Jesus had stolen the body, and thus the empty tomb was found. The inherent contradictions of this twisted approach apparently were forgotten by its early adherents; for if the enemies stole the body of Jesus, they could have displayed it at once on their own.

d) Probably the most popular denial of the resurrection stories rests in the "hallucination theory." This certainly pays tribute to the good faith and honesty of the disciples, but it holds that they were so overwrought by the pangs of losing their master when he appeared to be on the brink of success, that by a kind of group suggestion they imagined him to be again in their midst.

The hallucination theory overlooks the chronic and continual disbelief of the disciples, which runs through all the resurrection narratives. They practically ridicule the holy women with the first reports of having seen Jesus again, they state their scepticism again and again (and most explicity, in the words of Thomas), and they find that Jesus appears to them in no psychological pattern which could possibly be explained by a sort of group self-hypnosis.

What we have said above does not deny the fact that for us we find some difficulties in reconciling certain qualities of the gospel narratives. The answer, of course, is that the gospels merely hand on the traditions as they received them, not bothering to try to erase any apparent inconsistencies.

The most prominent difficulty is the tradition of appearances by Jesus only in the Jerusalem area, contrasted with the tradition that Jesus will meet his disciples again in Galilee. Also, you will note that the gospel of Mark has an incomplete ending: in verse 8 of chapter 16, we are merely told that the "women were afraid." Something has certainly been lost here. Some unknown hand finished Mark from verses 9 through 20, putting these lines together as a composite of stories in the other narratives.

You will also find in John's gospel that this gospel ends, as it were twice: first after chapter 20, and then after another episode in chapter 21. The expertly charming account of the seven men fishing on the lake of Galilee in chapter 21 reads as if practically no other apparitions of Jesus had occurred, since it calls this one "the third."

How many apparitions of Jesus are listed in the gospels and in St. Paul's account (1 Corinthians 15)? Depending on the analysis whether or not certain apparitions appear more than once with differing details, this number could be between six or seven up to thirteen.

You should remember that the "apparitions" are just that: appearances of Jesus. Theologically speaking, the ascension of Jesus, body and soul, to the right hand of God the Father occurred at the moment of the resurrection. After that moment, however, Jesus periodically made himself present in a physically visible form to the holy women and to the disciples. At some final date he visibly let them know that these "random" appearances of him in his glorified body would cease. This conclusion of his presence on earth is described for us in the terms of his visible ascension into the heavens.

THE ACTS OF THE APOSTLES

READ: as much of the Acts as you wish.

You should remember that the Acts of the Apostles was a book written by St. Luke as the complement of his gospel. It was intended to be read in connection with the gospel.

Strictly speaking, the book is misnamed, because it does not discuss the actions of all the apostles. Its first half is concerned with certain events in the life of the early church, emphasizing the role of Peter. Then, with the introduction of the story of the conversion of St. Paul, you will find Acts wholly concerned with the travelogue that gives you the outline of what have been called St. Paul's three missionary journies.

A knowledge of the geography of Asia Minor, Greece, and Italy would be helpful for you to follow Paul's journies. For this, you can use either illustrated slides or printed maps.

One characteristic of Acts which reflects ancient literary custom is Luke's insertion of lengthy speeches which appear to be far too long to have been uttered at the moment. One such example is the very diffuse sermon of St. Stephen in Chapter 7 at a time when his enemies are on the verge of stoning him to death. The general idea was that the person in question did not have to utter these exact words, but at a solemn moment the proper words for the occasion were to be put into his mouth. This was not deception; at least the nucleus of the ideas was his.

READ: Acts 1

This chapter includes Luke's account of a visible manifestation of Jesus whereby the disciples understood this would be the last time they would see him in his glorified body.

READ: Acts 2

Particularly in verse 42 to verse 47, you will read here an example of what have been called the "idyllic passages" in Acts. They give the impression of perfect saintly harmony in the early church, and they are not false in saying this, provided we understand that grave dissension also existed at the same time with this sense of Christian oneness. Acts itself gives testimony to the problems of the infant church. Its greatest problem was its identity crisis: Was it to be a branch of Judaism, as it were, accepting Jesus as the Messiah? Was it to retain or to discard practices of the Jewish law? Notice that there was no immediate unanimity on these points even among the leaders of the church.

READ: Acts 4, 32-36, and Acts 5, 1-11.

Here is another of the "idyllic passages." It is followed by a frightening account of the deaths of Ananias and Sapphira. The account was certainly interpreted in the early church as teaching a lesson, lest a member of the church lie to its overseers, perhaps; but the modern questions raised about this passage ask what was so grave a sin as to call down instant death in a matter which was originally voluntary: the ownership of property in common. It would appear that all we can conclude is that we are reading the interpretation accepted in the early church. We cannot read into this story any element of God's personal judgment on this couple.

READ: Acts 7

We have already mentioned the nature of Stephen's discourse before his death. You should notice the first appearance of Paul as "Saul" in verse 58.

READ: Acts 9

With this account of Saul's vision on the way to Damascus, you are beginning the biography of Paul as it appears in the New Testament.

READ: Acts 13, 14, 15

This is easy and interesting reading, particularly if you follow Paul's route on a map. Notice in Chapter 15, 37 that problems of the clash of personalities appear to have arisen between Paul and Barnabas because of some earlier action by John Mark, whose motivation is unknown to us but evidently displeasing to Paul.

READ: Acts 18, 24 following

Notice the mention here of Apollos, whose name will recur in Paul's admonition to the Corinthians not to break up into factions following Apollos or Paul or Peter, or supposedly "Christ." Apollos is also believed to be the author of the epistle to the Hebrews.

As you continue reading, you will undoubtedly notice (as in Chapter 20, verse 6) the references to "we." These are quite universally accepted as written by Luke in the first person plural to indicate that he was with Paul at all these times, and personally witnessed the events he describes in the "we" passages.

READ: Acts 27, 28

These are the closing portions of the travelogue that so many generations of readers have found so gripping in Acts. What intrigues our modern generation is the question why Acts ends where it does: Paul remains in prison in Rome. Why did Luke end his journal here? Did Luke consider that the gospel now had been adequately spread because it had reached Rome, the center of the world? No answer has been suggested which has been accepted as universally satisfactory.

It is generally accepted, however, that Paul was freed after this imprisonment in Rome. Perhaps he made another missionary journey to Spain. Early writers pass on the tradition that he was martyred at Rome in 67 A.D.

THE EPISTLES OF ST. PAUL

As outlined in the Introduction to this booklet, the comments given here are not intended to be detailed or complete commentaries on either the Hebrew Old or the Greek New Testament. They are rather formulated in order to be orientations, general attitudes, and suggestions for making the biblical reading more interesting.

This norm continues here in our comments on the epistles of St. Paul. Paul's personality is complex, his actions are those of a genius. However, even his outlook changed as he grew older. In his earlier years as a convert to Christ Jesus from the rabid persecutor he had been, he certainly shared the opinion prevalent in the early church, that the end of the world would come soon. How much this attitude colored the opinions voiced in his early epistles is argued by scholars; but we must admit that the belief in the forthcoming end of everything was part of his outlook. Only as the years progressed and history taught him its lesson did he realize that God's plan for the end was not yet.

Another distinction you should keep in mind is the difference between Paul's suggestions, his commands, his inculcation of contemporary customs, and his teaching of permanent Christian doctrine. This is an area of Pauline thinking which is receiving more attention in our day than previously. One reason is that occasionally a Pauline approach seems to run counter to a development sanctioned and encouraged in the present-day church.

The prime example which can come to mind is found in Paul's seventh chapter in his first epistle to the Corinthians. There he presents an exhortation to virginity as a higher state of life than marriage, in addition to recommending marriage for those who find sexual continence too difficult to observe. In the light of the teaching of the Second Vatican Council concerning the personalist purposefulness of marriage for the spouses concerned, Paul's wording as if marriage were primarily an outlet for concupiscence has come in for sharp criticism in our own day.

Did Paul give such advice as part of his belief that the end of the world was nigh? Did Paul reflect a reaction to pagan excesses at Corinth? Are Paul's opinions relevant only to times in the early church, not representing stable Christian doctrine in this connection? These are questions that have been raised in an issue like this.

Another example of the distinction between the customs of Paul's time and permanent Christian belief could be Paul's wish that women have their heads covered in church. The contemporary change in the status of women has been so drastic that the Pauline replies to the questions he received from the Corinthian church would seem to have lost most of their relevance for our own day. The equal education for modern women plus their ability to support themselves independently places them in a class utterly divorced from the status of the Christian women Paul knew at Corinth. Certainly, it would seem, Paul's rules for the women of Corinth should not be placed on a par with Paul's teaching concerning the Holy Eucharist or Paul's theology on the place of Jesus Christ as our Savior.

Still another area where misunderstanding occurred in the past (and could occur in your own mind) concerns Paul's use of the words "flesh" and "spirit." For Paul, "flesh" is not equated with the body, and "spirit" as something immaterial is not necessarily good. Instead, Paul uses "flesh" to refer to the negative, sinful tendencies of mankind; and "spirit" to refer to everything in us that wishes to turn to God. It would be a grievous mistake ever to think that Paul speaks of the body as sinful and the soul or spirit as good because it is immaterial. Paul is the first to make capital the point that the body should be the temple of the Holy Spirit, and therefore it should not be desecrated.

We shall select the greatest of St. Paul's epistles in the pages to come. For the moment, we should point out some of the questions regarding Pauline authorship of various epistles, even those we omit here for comment.

The twentieth-century version of "authorship" would not hold for the author of the epistles of St. Paul. Characteristically, a literary slave would do the writing, perhaps even choose words, at the behest of the "author," who would then accept the letter as his own and sign it with his own hand. But the question recurs: Did Paul write some of his epistles himself? Or did a secretary write them, following Paul's dictation verbatim? Or in others, were they composed by a disciple of Paul, so close to his master's thought that the thought is that of Paul, but the wording seems different?

There is no question here of denying that all these epistles are part of the New Testament, and that they are inspired like the rest of the bible. The question of their authorship, however, helps us to interpret their wording and to understand their implications and their references.

You should not be surprised to read of discussions on the points we mentioned above. You should realize further that not all of Paul's letters have been saved. For example, his epistles to the Corinthians clearly imply (1 Cor. 5, 9; 2 Cor. 2,4) that he had written other documents which we do not now possess. Some scholars even deduce that Paul's Second Letter to the Corinthians is a composite of more than one letter, which historically had been sent to all the churches at different times.

Finally, we should mention still another characteristic of the Pauline epistles. They are all incidental letters. They were written in response to a local need, in reply to a local question, to correct a local abuse. Paul himself could never have dreamed that some of his missives would have been saved so lovingly for all further Christian generations.

THE EPISTLE TO THE ROMANS

Before you read Romans, you should realize that no letter of Paul is so profound as this. Romans treats of ultimates; faith in God, the grace of God that justifies us, and the majesty of God that is so far beyond us. A danger can exist for scrupulous and worrisome persons who selectively remember only references to the wrath of God for damnation. If you are such, you should balance such fears with the reminder that the God of infinite justice is the God of infinite mercy. Paul, to be sure, makes it clear that God is the God of mercy as well as the God of justice, but not all Paul's readers have made this clear to themselves. And if you find yourself worrying about being justified in God's sight, you must balance that fact with the Pauline truth that the grace of God is freely given you in order to justify you in God's sight.

READ: samples or complete texts in the early chapters of Romans

You will shortly meet with Paul's references to the "wrath" or "anger" of God. Historically, these terms have been misunderstood as if God were some sort of avenging tyrant, full of malicious caprice against helpless mankind. They should be understood instead as the justifiable reaction (speaking in human terms) that God would have against all sin, all deliberate evil, all revolt of puny man making himself god against the one true God.

The "salvation by faith" theme which runs through Romans is a reaction against the belief that mere performance of religious actions (for example, the Jewish Law) was enough to justify oneself in God's sight. Paul is arguing instead, and correctly, that only the grace of God can justify us, since we have no power on the supernatural level to act as God. We obtain this grace and we obtain this justification by means of our faith in God, which in itself is already a grace offered to us, if only we are willing to accept it and cooperate with God's word.

Paul is also speaking like a rabbi of his times, using examples and texts from the Hebrew Testament to make his point. Thus, the faith of Abraham, who "hoped against hope" and believed in God's word even when all appearances were to the contrary, should be a model of our own faith in order to be justified.

In reading these pages of Romans, you must keep in mind that Paul is condemning an excess, namely, that mere observance of the Jewish Law is sufficient for salvation. Paul is arguing instead to the need for more than mere observance: the faith to vivify that observance.

Is this outlook insulting to Jewish belief? Absolutely not. The reason for this denial can be found in the following chapters:

READ: Romans 9; 10; 11

Some scripture scholars have proposed the opinion that the root theme in Romans is not salvation by faith but rather Paul's wrestling with the theological problem of the Chosen People. If God chose Israel as He did for all time, then how can God reject Israel after Israel has not accepted Jesus as Messiah?

This is the gist of these three chapters. You should particularly note (in 11, 16) how Paul emphasizes that Israel is the parent stock, and that the gentiles, the grafted branches, have no right to preen themselves as superior to Israel. The mercy of God, Paul insists, still holds true and will always hold true for Israel. In God's merciful providence Israel will somehow or other be saved as well.

These three chapters in Romans end with a doxology (a hymn of praise) which is among the most sublime prayers of adoration contained anywhere in the bible. Be sure you read it carefully in chapter 11, 33-36.

We should note here that Paul's Epistle to the Galatians is almost a parallel although much shorter treatment of the same themes (faith, justification and observance of the Law) as in Romans.

THE FIRST EPISTLE TO THE CORINTHIANS

This epistle is receiving, as we already stated, more and more criticism in our own day as being out of date and inapplicable to our changed times. Some of this disagreement seems to stem from ignorance of the audience for whom the epistle was intended. Corinth in Greece was notorious among Roman and Grecian cities for its utter immorality. Other pagan cities were bad enough; yet they considered Corinth worst for its depravity. The Christian community at Corinth deserves our sympathy for trying to make its way amid so discouraging an environment. It was at the bottom of the social ladder: substantially, a group of slaves. If the husbands in the Christian Corinthian church were uneducated slaves, we can gain some idea of the lack of education, social caste, and religious upbringing which would exist among their wives and their children.

This "first" epistle is "first" only in our records; there may have been more preceding it which have long been extinct. It represents Paul's answers to questions which have come to him, asking for directives; and Paul's reprimands to remove abuses of which he has heard. In that sense, some of the problems to which he addresses himself have long since passed off the scene, and First Corinthians can only give us a picture of the principles Paul applied to solve a difficulty which no longer exists for us.

READ: First Corinthians 1; 2; 3; 4

Paul begins by excoriating the Corinthian church for having factions existing within itself which destroy its unity in Christ. On this score, Paul is anything but out of date! The history of all Christendom repeatedly exemplifies the scandalous and sometimes even murderous divisions which have existed in the church of Christ, such as when the Crusaders of the Middle Ages butchered Jew, Moslem, and Christian indiscriminately.

READ: First Corinthians 5

Paul's condemnation of a man living with his mother-in-law was considered a condemnation of incest. Paul's advice (if not his command) to expel this Corinthian from the church was taken as a pattern in later ages for the church to excommunicate various members for serious infractions.

READ: First Corinthians 6

The question of the morality involved when a Christian had recourse to the pagan courts would be an example of a situation no longer relevant in our day. Paul's insistence, however, on the holiness of the body is badly needed in our day, in a world which laughs at sex as a bodily activity lacking human values.

READ: First Corinthians 7

Verse 15 in this chapter has been used by the church for long centuries as biblical authorization to dissolve the bond of a non-sacramental marriage when, after two unbaptized persons are married, one of them, becoming a Christian, is baptized and the unbaptized partner refuses to live peaceably in marriage with the convert. This has been called the "Pauline Privilege."

(Further comments on the difficulties of reconciling some of Paul's wording here with the union of spouses idealized in modern Catholic attitudes were already mentioned in our introduction to St. Paul on page 109)

READ: First Corinthians 8; 9; 10

For the Corinthians, a grave problem existed as to the morality of buying and then eating food which had been sacrificed to idols in the pagan temples. This is a problem hardly existing anywhere in the world in our day.

READ: First Corinthians 11

The many references here to the dress of women at Corinth must certainly be considered relevant only to that day and place. We must remember that the decent woman would never go out in public with her head uncovered; her head was to be uncovered only to her husband, and that at home. Prostitutes regularly appeared in public unveiled, as a sign of their availability.

Scripture commentators are hard put to give an accepted explanation for Paul's statement that women should have their heads covered "out of respect for the angels" (First Corinthians 11, 10). Paul is arguing rabbinically from Genesis when he says that "woman was created for the sake of man." And if it appears that Paul is criticizing only the woman, in fairness we should note that Paul also says that "long hair on a man is nothing to be admired"! (First Corinthians 11, 14)

Versus 17 through 22 in this eleventh chapter offer us one of the most precious doctrinal and liturgical testimonies extant from the early church. We must place the date of this epistle at perhaps 57 A.D., as one of the earliest documents we possess regarding Christian belief and practice, and certainly anteceding all the gospels. Here Paul recites the tradition concerning the Last Supper and the institution of the Holy Eucharist. If First Corinthians gave us nothing more than these six verses, it would already be a priceless testimonial.

READ: First Corinthians 12

This chapter lists various gifts of the spirit, commonly called *charismata.* Paul gives all credit to God from whom all gifts come, and warns that any of these gifts can be misused unless they are put at the disposal of the church, for the good of the community in accord with right order. Paul's comparison of the various functions of the parts of the body whereby the body needs all of its parts, and no part has the right to hold itself above the others, has passed into tradition its application to the church as the mystical body of Christ.

READ: First Corinthians 13

Verses 1 through 13 are listed repeatedly among the world's greatest literature. No comment here can improve here on Paul's genius in his description of perfect charity, perfect love. You should recognize this passage for what it is: a superlative tribute to love.

READ: First Corinthians 14

Paul returns now to the subject of the charismatic gifts, emphasizing that they are subject to regulation by the church community. "I would rather say five words that mean something than ten thousand words in a tongue" (First Corinthians 14, 19). Evidently abuses had occurred on this point. The strictures of Paul then, appear thoroughly pertinent in our own day as well.

READ: First Corinthians 15

As if the testimony of the institution of the Holy Eucharist were not enough, coupled with the unsurpassed lyric tribute to true love, Paul now gives us a third gem: his summary of the tradition concerning the apparitions of Jesus after the resurrection, in addition to Paul's defense of the resurrection of the body as an imitation of the resurrection of Jesus. As you read these lines, notice the connotation throughout. Paul does not feel that he has to defend the truth of the resurrection of Jesus; that is accepted and taken for granted. It is the glorified resurrection of the individual body that is being defended since that is what the Corinthians denied.

In verse 35, Paul gives answers which are as valid today as they were in 57 A.D.: "What sort of body do these people have when they come back, raised from the dead?" His reply: "These are stupid questions."

THE SECOND EPISTLE TO THE CORINTHIANS

READ: selections or all of this letter, as you wish; but in particular Chapters 10, 11, and 12.

We have already indicated that Paul must have written more than the two letters we possess to the Christian community at Corinth. The special interest of our "Second Epistle" lies in the fact that fragments of one or more of these lost letters are contained in it, perhaps having been inserted at a later date when Paul's letters were being passed to other churches.

You yourself can discern with no trouble that chapters 10, 11, and 12 are very strong in their language. Most of the epistle is concerned with the subject of reconciliation between Paul and the community, but these chapters rather abruptly move into a position that hardly brooks compromise.

We must understand the local situation. Paul faced defiance, perhaps open rebellion. The opposition was so strong that Paul could only appeal to his complete dedication to his apostolate, and let the facts speak for themselves. He could hardly be justly accused of self-seeking if the supposed occasion for that self-seeking—his apostolate—brought on him so much suffering and failure.

It is in chapter 12 that he hints of some special mystical experience God gave him to buoy him up in his suffering. The famous reference in verse 7 of this chapter to his "sting" or "thorn" of the flesh indicates that God also permitted some special cross to be part of his life, for God's own purposes. Just what this "sting of the flesh" was, no one knows. The list of possibilities is relatively long, and practically all have been discarded to some extent so that no universal agreement has been reached as to the meaning of the reference. The "sting" was apparently something special to Paul. It could hardly have been strong sexual desire, for that reason. Was it a disgusting eye disease, which made his eye-lids swollen and scaly, such as could easily happen in his times? Was it stuttering, short stature, even baldness or bow legs? All have been suggested. One theory which has gained more probability is that Paul's rejection by the Jews, his brothers according to the flesh, was the "sting." Very low in acceptability should be rated the theory that Paul was an epileptic, and epileptic seizures were the "sting." The reason such seizures should be rejected is that this theory is based on the belief that Paul's conversion-experience on the road to Damascus was nothing but an epileptic seizure, when he would have seen the colored lights which typically accompany the disturbance of the brain centers.

THE EPISTLE TO THE EPHESIANS (and COLOSSIANS)

READ: selections or the complete texts of these two epistles, and note how often they resemble each other, almost word for word.

In particular, compare Ephesians 5, 21 through 6, 9 with Colossian 3, 5 through 4, 6. You will note in these lines how the image of the relationship of husband and wife approaches so much more closely the "personalist" outlook on Christian marriage than does the treatment of this subject in the seventh chapter of Corinthians. It is a particularly sublime comparison to urge husbands and wives to model their union on the union between Jesus Christ and his church.

Notice also how in these passages Paul, much like Jesus in the gospels, takes slavery for granted as a social institution. Paul, like Jesus, urges fair treatment of slaves. Nowhere, however, does one find even a hint that the existence of slavery as such was to be looked on as a social evil violating human rights. You might stop to reflect at some length on this fact. Could it be that slavery in itself could be a benign institution, depending on the master? We know from history that freedmen who had incurred heavy debts often enough sold themselves into slavery as a worthwhile solution to their problem.

THE EPISTLE TO THE PHILIPPIANS

This short letter is one of the most delightful and personal letters we possess from Paul's hand. The very special passage you should note in it is Chapter 2, verses 6 through 11. This is a hymn to the divinity of Jesus, as divine son of God the father. We have no way of knowing whether Paul himself was the author of the hymn. It seems more likely that Paul is quoting this hymn here from an early christian liturgy.

THE PASTORAL EPISTLES
(FIRST AND SECOND TO TIMOTHY; TO TITUS)

These three short letters are worth reading for their testimony to customs in the early church and social customs from their times as well.

Their style is very different from the other letters of Paul, but the thought is thoroughly Pauline. The explanation of the differences seems to lie in the fact that Paul gave these ideas to some secretary, perhaps a disciple, perhaps even to Luke the evangelist, who selected the phraseology.

Note specially in the First Letter to Timothy in chapter 2, verses 9 through 15 and 5, verses 3 through 16, the Pauline thought concerning married women and widows, whether in their private lives or acting as church servants ("deaconnesses"). The opening verses of chapter 6 repeat ideas concerning slavery already found in earlier epistles.

THE EPISTLE TO THE HEBREWS

READ: Selections or the entire epistle, as you wish. Note in particular Chapter 10, verses 26 through 31.

The history of this New Testament letter is quite singular. Even from early centuries in the church, there was doubt that the tradition of Pauline authorship was accurate. The thought was certainly related to that of St. Paul, but the vocabulary and literary style were recognized as completely different. Even more, the method of quoting the Hebrew Testament followed different lines compared to St. Paul.

Modern thought, although not absolutely certain, favors the attribution of authorship to Apollos, the Jew from Alexandria mentioned in Acts 18, 24, who was also claimed by a faction of the church at Corinth as their leader.

This epistle experienced still another rather singular development in its history. Groups of rigorists appealed to it in early Christianity as support of their view that certain sins could not be forgiven after one repentance, or even not forgiven at all. They referred to quotations from sections like chapter 10, verse 31, "It is a dreadful thing to fall into the hands of the living God." We ourselves should recall that no one, even the holiest of all human beings, can stand up to the infinite holiness and perfection of God. The grace of God is needed by all, saints no less than sinners; and it is utterly fallacious to dream that human creatures can become so virtuous as to be worthy, short of receiving God's grace, of God's holiness. Because of this rigoristic use Hebrews was temporarily in disfavor in the church.

Hebrews, however, has notable teaching value for us today. The letter was apparently addressed to Jewish Christians. It was perhaps written as early as the years before 70 A.D., when the temple was destroyed at Jerusalem. It exemplifies a typical Jewish method of quoting scripture, in its repeated appeals to the Hebrew Testament. This outlook is not such a one as we would favor in our times; but we can learn from Hebrews how biblical texts would be joined in order to prove or exemplify a point.

THE LETTER OF JAMES

READ: all of James

The Letter of James is included among the seven short missives at the end of the New Testament. These letters for many centuries have been called "Catholic," from the Greek word for "universal," since they were evidently addressed at one time to all the Christian churches or communities.

Who is this author? He is usually accepted as James, the "brother of the Lord" mentioned in Matthew 13, 55 and Acts 12, 17. He is certainly not the apostle James, the son of Zebedee and brother of John. Nor does he seem to be the other apostle named James, who was the son of Alpheus. As head of the early Christian community at Jerusalem, he had a close relationship with converts to Christianity from Judaism. The present letter clearly is intended for such an audience.

Nevertheless, the short treatise is more of a sermon than a letter. It specifically emphasizes the need for good works, and bitterly attacks the misuse of riches and the oppression of the poor.

Why was it written? One theory holds that certain Christians over-reacted to Paul's emphasis on faith in Romans and in Galatians. Later, James would see the necessity of reminding them that faith must lead to good works, just as Paul earlier had taught that good works lacking faith are useless. It would appear to be far-fetched to claim that James wrote this letter in order to attack Paul and Paul's doctrine on the necessity of faith.

You should especially notice the verses in chapter 5, 14-16. These sentences were cited by the Council of Trent as teaching the existence of the sacrament of the sick (formerly called Last Anointing or Extreme Unction).

No biblical work in either of the testaments surpasses James in strictures on social injustice. What the prophet Amos did for the Hebrew Testament, James has done for the New.

THE BOOK OF REVELATION (APOCALYPSE)

READ: selections or as much as you wish.

We began this simplified biblical commentary with emphasis on the necessity of understanding the literary form of a biblical text in order to understand the text itself. We end it now, on the same note and with more emphasis, if possible. The book of Revelation is an apocalypse ("revelation" is the English translation of the Greek word "apocalypse"). It has been variously called the most confusing book in the New Testament, the most obscure, the most difficult to understand. The reason for this rather unanimous judgment lies in its type of literary form: apocalyptic.

Apocalyptic writing appeared (as we noted earlier) in the Hebrew Testament, and became more and more popular as the Christian era approached. This kind of writing in the bible has several clearly defined characteristics, and they appear even more clearly in this book of Revelation:

a) apocalyptic claims to be a type of prophecy;

b) written after the event, but often projected into the future;

c) most of all, highly symbolic, even to the point of an allegorical meaning for each and every detail, if not each and every word at times;

d) with an unusually frequent use of symbolic numbers;

e) and usually with anonymous or pseudonymous authorship. This means that the book is attributed to someone else, as pseudonymous.

The authorship of Revelation remains controverted. Its author claims to be named John—but which John? Most probably, this is John the apostle, writing in his old age; but it could be someone named John the Elder, or another Christian disciple named John.

What complicates the authorship question even more is the probability that Revelation has been compiled from at least two earlier apocalypses. The reason for this opinion is the fact that one series of texts in Revelation seems to refer to the reign of Nero, before 70 A.D., and another series seems to refer to the reign of Domitian in about 95.

To understand something of the symbolism of numbers, you must remember that "7" is arbitrarily taken as a perfect number, as is also "3" to a lesser extent. Multiples of the perfect number can indicate "perfect perfection," such as "777." Thus, if this perfect number is made to lose its perfection three times (i.e. by reducing 7 to 6, thrice), then "666" can symbolize perfect imperfection, or complete evil—the "number of the beast," as in Revelation's chapter 13, verse 18.

The most important factor to remember in reading the book of Revelation is that it should never be taken in its strictly and slavishly literal sense. Even the first three chapters, consisting of letters to the seven churches of Asia Minor have their share of symbolism, in extending the warning against Gnostic heresy to all parts of the Christian world.

The main thrust of the book of Revelation, however, is certainly directed against Rome—the beast. The seven hills of Rome are mentioned in symbol, as are ten subordinate kingdoms, and continuing details.

The value of apocalyptic writing was that it encouraged the faithful Christians to persevere, even though the pagan aggressor seemed to be all-powerful. God in his own time would intervene, and if God did not intervene, none the less God was permitting this evil persecution to continue for good purposes known only to God. By the fact that apocalyptic is written in cipher, as it were, known only to the initiated Christians, it could be more bold in denouncing the reigning Roman emperors without being accused before them of treason and rebellion.

THE BACKGROUND
OF THE BIBLE
Rome
Thessalonica
Philippi
Corinth
Athens
Malta
Crete
Mediterr
S

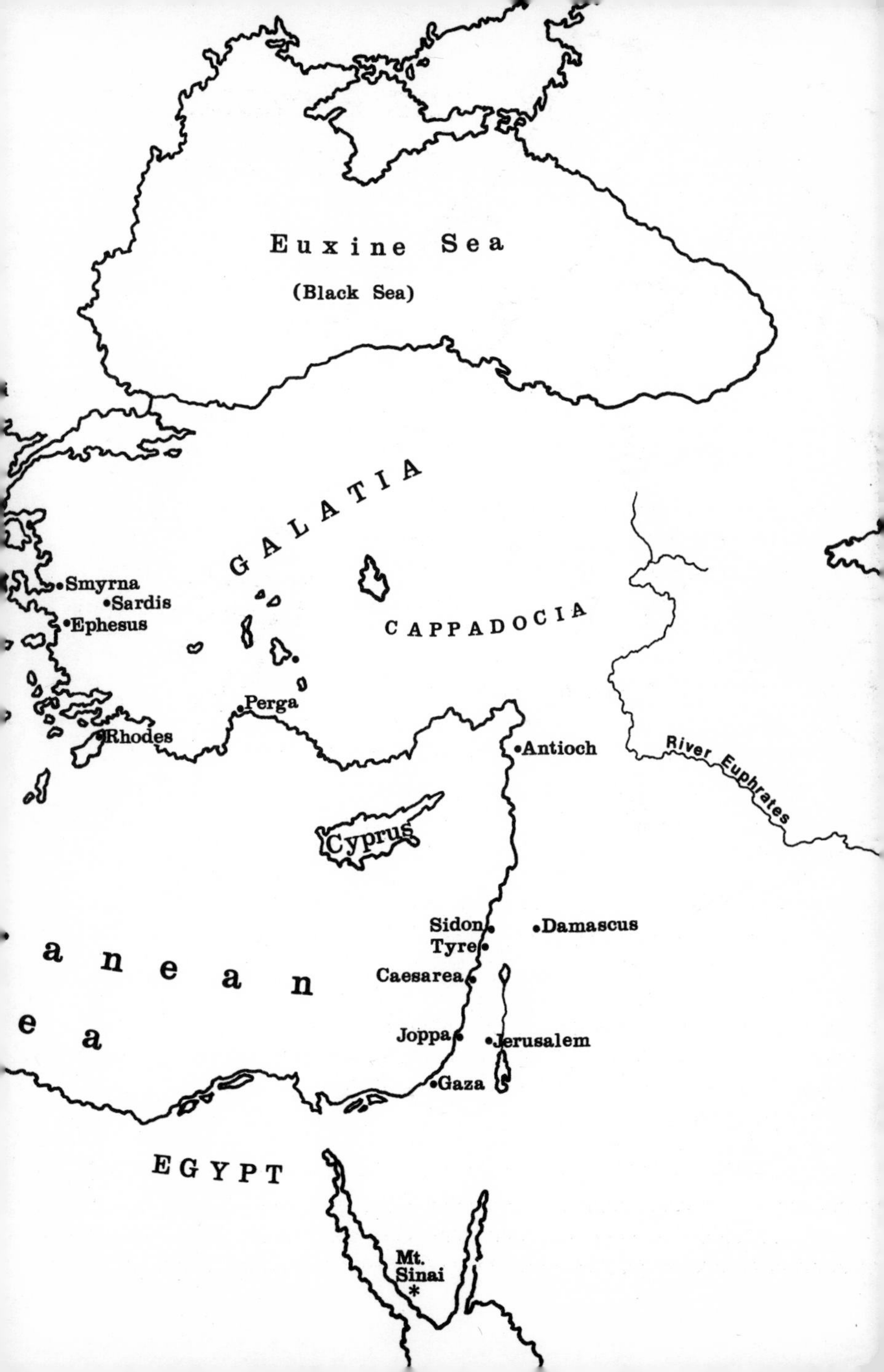

Euxine Sea
(Black Sea)
GALATIA
Smyrna
Sardis
Ephesus
CAPPADOCIA
Perga
Rhodes
Antioch
River Euphrates
Cyprus
Sidon
Damascus
Tyre
Caesarea
a n e a n
e a
Joppa
Jerusalem
Gaza
EGYPT
Mt.
Sinai

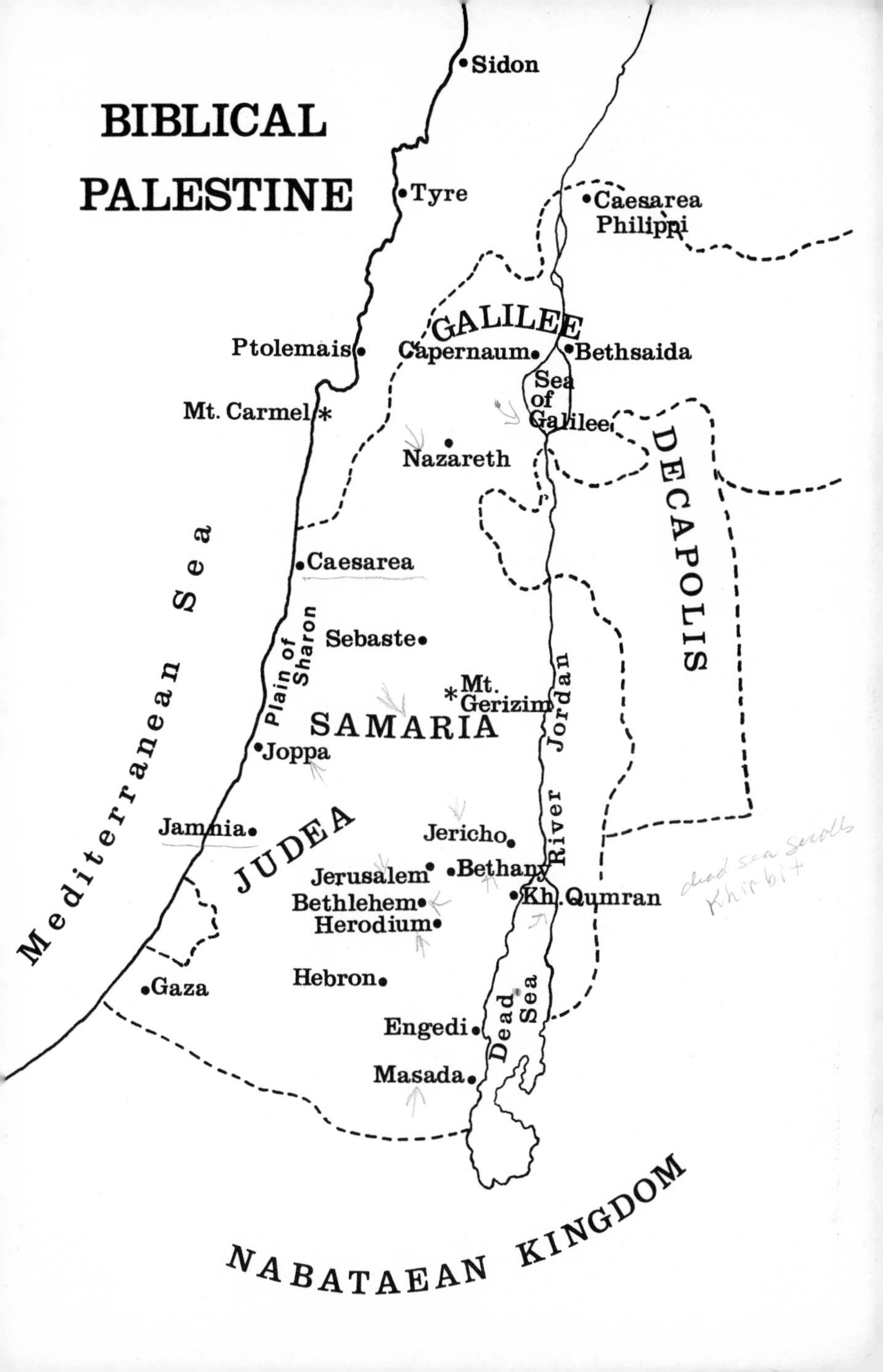
BIBLICAL PALESTINE
Sidon
Tyre
Caesarea Philippi
GALILEE
Ptolemais
Capernaum
Bethsaida
Sea of Galilee
Mt. Carmel
Nazareth
DECAPOLIS
Mediterranean Sea
Caesarea
Plain of Sharon
Sebaste
Mt. Gerizim
SAMARIA
Jordan River
Joppa
Jamnia
JUDEA
Jericho
Jerusalem
Bethany
Kh. Qumran
dead sea scrolls
Khirbit
Bethlehem
Herodium
Gaza
Hebron
Engedi
Dead Sea
Masada
NABATAEAN KINGDOM

NOTES

NOTES

Cogan Productions distributes the following Filas filmstrips which can be used as supplements to the material in this book:

LITERARY FORMS: A KEY TO UNDERSTAND THE BIBLE
BIBLICAL LOCATIONS IN JERUSALEM—TODAY
JERUSALEM, 66 A.D.
BIBLICAL LOCATIONS IN GALILEE—TODAY
THE DESERTS OF BIBLICAL ISRAEL—TODAY
THE SEACOAST OF THE BIBLE—TODAY
THE SHROUD OF TURIN: IS THIS THE PHOTOGRAPH OF JESUS CHRIST?
THE RESURRECTION OF JESUS
PLACES PAUL VISITED, AS THEY LOOK TODAY
1978 EXPOSITION OF THE SHROUD OF TURIN
WHERE JESUS LIVED— AS IT LOOKS TODAY

For more information, write to: